MW00806041

*"If my words did glow /
with the gold of sunshine /
And my tunes were played /
on a harp unstrung /
Would you hear my voice /
come through the music /
would you hold it near /
as it were your own?"*

From "Ripple" 1970
by Robert Hunter and Jerry Garcia

Golden Wisdom from the Grateful Dead:

Life Lessons in their Songs

by
Charles Beard

Golden Wisdom from the Grateful Dead: Life Lessons in their Songs
Copyright © 2023 by Finger of Fate LLC.

All rights reserved. No part of this book may be reproduced or used in any manner without written permission of the copyright owner.

Paperback Edition: Finger of Fate LLC, Austin, Tx.
ISBN 979-8-218-30424-9

Credits: Photographs & images are protected by copyright law. Resale or use of any images of this book is prohibited.

Cover ©Sakuraco & saginowski /Adobe Stock /stock.adobe.com
Numerous Interior Images ©/Adobe Stock /stock.adobe.com

Grateful Dead Photos

Grateful Dead St. Louis Armory May 1968. ©Tom Tussey tusseyphoto.com-
Robert Hunter ©Jay Blakesberg www.blakesberg.com
Jerry Garcia ©Chris Stone gratefulphoto.com
Grateful Dead at the Warfield, 1980 ©Chris Stone gratefulphoto.com

Song Lyrics

THAT'S IT FOR THE OTHER ONE (III. THE OTHER ONE)
Words and Music by BOB WEIR and BILL KREUTZMANN
© 1968 (Renewed) ICE NINE PUBLISHING CO., INC.
All Rights Reserved
Used by Permission of ALFRED MUSIC

RIPPLE LOSER
BLACK PETER
Words by ROBERT HUNTER Music by JERRY GARCIA
© 1971 (Renewed) ICE NINE PUBLISHING CO., INC.
All Rights Reserved
Used by Permission of ALFRED MUSIC

TRUCKIN'
Words by ROBERT HUNTER
Music by JERRY GARCIA, BOB WEIR and PHIL LESH
© 1971, 1973 (Renewed) ICE NINE PUBLISHING CO., INC.
All Rights Reserved
Used by Permission of ALFRED MUSIC

SCARLET BEGONIAS
U.S. BLUES
Words by ROBERT HUNTER Music by JERRY GARCIA
© 1974 (Renewed) ICE NINE PUBLISHING CO., INC.
All Rights Reserved
Used by Permission of ALFRED MUSIC

TOUCH OF GREY
Words by ROBERT HUNTER Music by JERRY GARCIA
© 1984 ICE NINE PUBLISHING CO., INC.
All Rights Reserved
Used by Permission of ALFRED MUSIC

HELP ON THE WAY FRANKLIN'S TOWER
Words by ROBERT HUNTER Music by JERRY GARCIA
© 1975 ICE NINE PUBLISHING CO., INC.
All Rights Reserved
Used by Permission of ALFRED MUSIC

CRYPTICAL ENVELOPMENT
Words and Music by JERRY GARCIA
© 1971 (Renewed) ICE NINE PUBLISHING CO., INC.
All Rights Reserved

Contents

Dedication

This book is dedicated to Angela, Jennifer and Crystal. I love you more than words can tell.

Prologue

"If my words did glow with the gold of sunshine"

From "Ripple" 1970
by Robert Hunter and Jerry Garcia

In the later half of the twentieth century, the traditional

social fabric of American life imploded. The "duck and cover"

childhood of us baby boomers, the Kennedy assassination, the

Vietnam War, racial and sexual inequality, environmental issues,

and even propaganda regarding reefer madness, caused a

loss of faith in the establishment. As a result many young

boomers sought truth and inspiration not in the Bible or religious

creeds, national allegiance, or family traditions as had previous

generations. Instead, popular media and especially music,

provided guideposts to life's most relevant and perplexing

questions.

Like many others, I found words of wisdom in popular music that blasted free on the radio or was available at the local record stores. The latest record release from my favorite groups was anticipated like a new sacred revelation passed down from Mt. Sinai. Music mattered. Between commercial DJ jabber, trendy hits on the radio dial revealed life changing lyrics in the songs of some truly classic recordings. I was thirteen years old in 1965, when I first heard the Rolling Stones play "Satisfaction" on the A.M. radio. I remember the words:

> "When I'm watchin' my TV / And a man comes on
> and tells me / How white my shirts can be / But,
> he can't be a man 'cause he doesn't smoke / The
> same cigarettes as me."

That anti-establishment (anti-consumerist) expression made a deep groove in my young mind at the time. Maybe much of the stuff spilling from my family's chatter box (TV) really was useless claptrap as Mick Jagger protested. Partially due to that song, becoming a Marlboro Man never appealed to me.

In my teenage garage band, we covered the Yardbirds' song, "Mister, You're a Better Man than I" (1965). The song condemned judging someone by the way he wears his hair. Because I had a mop top at the time, that made perfect sense to me. But, the song went on to equate that unfairness with judging people for the color of their skin. That lyric pushed me to see both forms of discrimination as unjust at an early age.

During this time the music and the words of Bob Dylan were blowing in the wind and heralded that the times really were *"a-changin."* The Beatles represented the pinnacle of the era's youth culture and served as the bell-bottomed gurus for my generation. Like millions of others, I embraced their message exemplified by their 1967 song, "All You Need is Love." If authenticity and truth were devoid in the previous factories of socialization, it came in the music of the baby boomer generation.

Today, I still find music to be a source of wisdom and inspiration. Naturally over the years, my tastes evolved and expanded since my early teens. I now appreciate lots of different sounds from different eras, cultures, and genres. Yet, music still matters, playing a major role in my life. Music can enlighten, entertain, and enrapture me to this day. Chills up my spine still happen occasionally. Yet, the music of the American band, the Grateful Dead, has resonated with me like no other. For many years, I have marveled at the songs of Robert Hunter (the main lyricist) and Jerry Garcia (the lead guitar player and singer). Their songs became more profound as they aged with me like precious metal. They have reverberated over decades. I believe many of their songs will eventually enter the Great American Songbook. Others have recognized the profound and prolonged impact of the band. Hundreds of books and thousands of articles have been written about the Grateful Dead. Why have I chosen to write another? As that truth seeking child of the '60s, I have found precious and golden wisdom within their music.

Do I have any special relationship with the band members? No. Although, I have met a couple of them at public gatherings, they don't know me from Adam. To the band members, I am one of the millions of people who have been struck by the uncommon artistic output of the band. I am just an aging fanboy, a self appointed Dead Head. My credentials do not come from selling grilled cheese or tie dyes while touring on the trail of the Grateful Dead. Instead, I have just been a fan for a very long time. I became a life-long aficionado relatively early in 1968 when the band came to my midwestern home town. I saw them when.... long before the invention of the steal your face logo (skull and lightning bolt), the demise of their original frontman (Pigpen), stadium size crowds, corporate concert sponsorship, hundred dollar tickets, and even the advent of the term "Dead Head." I have remained a fan since that first encounter, well over 50 years now. Very few things in my life have lasted as long. I never met Jerry Garcia or Robert Hunter—although each had a major impact on my life.

In my writing, I try not to put words in their mouths, but instead to quote them from their own thoughts and words from many publicly published sources that are usually footnoted.

Some Grateful Dead fans may be disappointed that this book is as much about me as it is the lyrics of Dead tunes. I have tried to indicate how the lyrics have touched me—how they made me think, feel, and act. Hopefully, my experiences will be relatable to many of other fans who have been exposed to the same music. However, my interpretation of the meaning and impact of these lyrics is solely my own. Others may hear the words differently and attribute their own contrasting meaning to them. That is really ok with me! It appears this laissez-faire approach to interpretation is congruent with the ethos of the band.

Much has been made about the intentional ambiguities the song writers built into the lyrics written for the Grateful Dead. Dead Heads, like me, often quote theses lyrics much like some cite the Bible or other holy books. Likewise, we can usually find a lyric that is appropriate for almost any of life's circumstances. But to prevent wild-eyed, psychedelic, estimated prophets (like Charlie Manson), from spinning off the planet with contrived hermeneutics, the writers agreed to avoid words that could be used to form a new quasi-religious creed. Perhaps other than an affirmative response to the question *"Whoa, oh, what I want to know is, are you kind?"* ("Uncle John's Band"), there are no discrete formulas or shibboleths for what Dead Heads must believe to join the party. The end result is a collection of lyrics that is open-ended and free from credos. According to Garcia, *"We don't sit around and work out Grateful Dead dogma, or catma if you prefer (laughs). Our trip is that everyone is entitled to believe what they want."*[1] Most often their words are simultaneously as obscure as a cloudy day and as illuminating as a ray of sunshine.[2]

Even the song writers resisted official interpretations of their words and allowed the lyrics to take on a life of their own in the minds of the listeners. In the preface of Robert Hunter's anthology of his songs, he explained, *"My versions of these songs are no more 'the real ones' than those that may have spoken to you through the music darkly some twenty years ago"* (Hunter, 1993, p. 2). It is noteworthy that his songs have stuck around far beyond his view of *"twenty years ago."* Garcia also confirmed, *"I'd rather the listener take the responsibility for interpreting the lyrics, that takes the responsibility off me."*[4] Therefore, I am thankful to be granted opportunity to interpret these songs for myself. The songwriters have allowed this

Life Lessons in their Songs

listener to hear important personal messages and find valuable and sometimes universal life lessons in their songs.

With my permission slip in hand, I have chosen to write about eleven lessons from ten Grateful Dead songs. The first chapter on "That's It for the Other One," describes my original psychedelic encounter with the band and the resulting head spinning repercussions. Next, spirituality is affirmed by the existence of a fountain not made by human hands (Robert Hunter's favorite line) in the song "Ripple."[5] The third chapter deals with a phrase from "Truckin'." It explores the message of the natural fluctuating nature of life when sometimes the light shines on us and other times we are immersed in darkness. "Help is on It's Way" is used to discuss the importance of improvisation in our every step. Our personal view point can sometimes allow us to see light in unexpected places according to next song, "Scarlet Begonias." The song "Loser" is an important reminder that not all folks have our best interests at heart. Beware of con men! "U.S. Blues" has encouraged me to have an open-eyed patriotism and an appreciation of the powerful inclusive nature of the band. The only song that Robert Hunter ever publicly interpreted is discussed in the chapter on "Franklin's Tower." That song has instilled in me the importance of listening to the music during times of confusion.

Another dip into the song "Truckin'" has helped me to view life as a long and strange trip, indeed. The message of "Black Peter" has given me a realistic and profound view of my own mortality. And finally "Touch of Grey" inspires an attitude of resilience in order to make the long-haul in this life.

All of these songs from the unlikely source of an American rock and roll band have helped provide essential life lessons. Yet, I believe that I have just scratched the surface of the wisdom of the band with these selected songs. The lyrics that follow are just the low-hanging fruit. Easy pickings! There is much more to be gleaned from their music than written about here. I am often surprised how many Grateful Dead songs not mentioned in this book grow and evolve with nuance and meaning over time. Hopefully this book will inspire you to listen more closely to the full body of music from this remarkable band.

Most of the lyrics mentioned here have been written by Robert Hunter. He was the elusive shadow lyricist of the band who stayed in the background and chafed at the star spotlight. Yet, he was inducted into the Rock and Roll Hall of Fame in 1994 along with the Grateful Dead. At the time, he was the first non-performing member of a band to be so honored. After his death, Hunter was recognized by *Rolling Stone Magazine* as, *"one of rock's most ambitious and dazzling lyricists who was literary counterpoint to the band's musical experimentation."*[6]

Hunter's songs, put to melody by Jerry Garcia, have captured my imagination the most in the Grateful Dead repertoire. Bill (the drummer) Kreutzmann also concurred regarding that selection of songs, *"Jerry Garcia's music with Robert Hunter's lyrics was the best of what we had to offer."*[7] I agree. But, I am well aware that nearly a dozen other lyricists contributed great songs to their catalog of original music. Special mention must go to Bob Weir and his writing buddy John Perry Barlow (quite the renaissance man). They too created some impressive songs for the band. However, Barlow explained his song writing role in the afterword of *The Complete Annotated Grateful Dead Lyrics*:

> *"Had it not been for me, and my other junior-varsity colleagues, this ecosystem you behold here would have been a monoculture, a brilliant garden in which all the flowers were roses but which lacked in the diversity that is essential to eco-logical health."*[8]

As such, I appreciate the diverse and colorful assortment of songs that bloomed from the light of all the other lyricists. Yet, it is the songs of varsity team, Hunter and Garcia, that shine the brightest. As Hunter suggested, many of the words discussed here do actually, *"glow with the gold of sunshine"* ("Ripple").

I hope that the songs mentioned in this book provide some helpful light and wisdom for your life as they have for mine.

Life Lessons in their Songs

Chapter 1

"The bus came by and I got on, that's when it all began /
There was Cowboy Neal at the wheel of a bus to never-ever land"

From "That's It for the Other One" 1968
by Bob Weir and Bill Kreutzmann

The lyrics above come from a 1967-68 trippy composition titled "That's It for the Other One" ("The Other One") written by Bob Weir and Bill Kreutzmann. Musically the tune, with a galloping 12/8 time signature, was a launching pad for explosive improvisation. Most often, it was a ten-minute or more instrumental piece punctuated with few verses and words. As one of the Grateful Dead's hardest driving tunes it was a drummer's showpiece. It resulted in many musical crescendos, which often sounded similar to a barreling freight train coming right at me. The exciting fan favorite, "The Other One" was played in concert over 500 times throughout the band's career.

With drums and bass locked into its locomotive beat, today I believe this tune is deeply embedded into my DNA.

Art reflects some incorrigible counterculture history in the background to this music. In the summer of 1964, Ken Kesey, the author of *One Flew Over the Cuckoo's Nest,* and his crew dubbed the "Merry Pranksters" traveled across the United States in an old day-glow painted school bus affectionately named "Furthur." That name indicated the general psychic mindset of the Pranksters. The LSD fueled escapades of those beatniks and proto-hippies were chronicled in Tom Wolfe's famous nonfiction work titled *The Electric Kool-aid Acid Test.* On the Merry Pranksters' festive road trip, Kesey declared "*Now, you're either on the bus or off the bus,*" as an effort to herd his fellow stoned and stray sojourners (Wolfe, 1968, p. 83).

Eventually as contemporaries and friends, members of the Grateful Dead were literally on THAT BUS, along with author Ken Kesey, bus driver Neal Cassady, and other legends known among later Dead Heads. The song "The Other One" is an ode to the Merry Pranksters and their high jinks. It is a cartoon-like narration of Bob Weir's psychedelic experiences with a Spanish lady ("*she lays on me this rose*"), the San Francisco cops who ("*busted me for smiling on a cloudy day*"), and a trip on "Furthur" with ("*Cowboy Neal at the wheel / on the bus to never-ever-land*").

Kesey's phrase *"on the bus"* coined for the original bus passengers on Furthur, eventually evolved to become a much broader metaphor. Those tuned into the Grateful Dead and a psychedelic revolution sweeping the youth culture of the day were considered *"on"* the celebrated bus.

In 1968 towards the end of my junior year in high school, there was a rumor that a San Francisco band was coming to St. Louis for a concert. The Grateful Dead was headed my way. They were going to play two nights in a big warehouse (the National Guard Armory) in downtown St. Louis. That was a pretty odd place for a concert—it was a big concrete building, which held the military weapons for the Missouri National Guard. Later lyrics described the local armory "*With a basement full of dynamite and live artillery*" ("One More Saturday Night"). This location for a rock concert was strange given the flower power vibe of the day. I wasn't a fan of the Grateful Dead at the time. I'd heard their first album and thought it sounded pretty rushed and thin musically. All my

friends were going to see and hear the Grateful Dead. A ticket

cost only $3.00 for the show. So I was ready to go.

$3 Ticket for First Grateful Dead concert--such a deal!

Between 1966-68, Bob Dylan, the Beatles, the Yardbirds,

and the Who had all come to play in my home town. I had

seen them all. But, a news report on the local TV station said

St. Louis was being visited by a West Coast, hippie band, the

Grateful Dead. On that broadcast I saw the first male I'd ever

seen with a pony tail. The Grateful Dead was in town! These

guys were not pretty boys like the Beatles (except for Bob Weir).

They looked scruffy, to say the least, downright menacing

might be a better description. The lead singer (Pigpen) was

especially formidable. He looked like a mean biker with a bad

attitude. Their lead guitar player (Jerry Garcia) was no more

attractive. He was stocky, had a prominent nose, frizzy hair,

and a bad complexion. He had no beard at this time. But, from their first album, he had the reputation as being "Captain Trips" (his Prankster name) and the defacto leader of the band. These guys looked like the kind of people my parents had warned me about. They weren't wearing flowers in their hair and they didn't appear to be all "peace and love."

Original Handbill for First St. Louis Concert.

A small group of people came out for the concert. There was no mass appeal for the band in the Midwest at the time, at least in St. Louis in 1968. There weren't many people in town who knew anything about the Grateful Dead at the time and there were fewer who cared. No more than a couple of hundred people showed up. This was quite a contrast to their huge crowds in later years. Those who came out were a certain hip intelligentsia, at least my high school buddies and I fancied ourselves as part of such a group—despite the fact we were really just high school teeny boppers. My closest pals and I were all present that evening to hear the Grateful Dead's first concert in our home town. The guy who actually produced the show, Jorge Martinez, recalled the following

> "They charged $3,000 a night, and with the extra production costs - like renting the hall, and a big Wurlitzer organ for 'Pigpen,' who was with them then - it came to about 10 grand. Almost nobody here had heard of the Dead," said Martinez, now a designer of furniture and other household objects. "The first night we sold about 125 tickets. The second night, about 250. So we ended up selling around 375 tickets at $3 apiece." You can't make money that way, as Martinez discovered. But most of those who attended had fun, "just tripping around on the floor because there were no seats," Martinez recalled. St Louis Post-Dispatch (MO)[2]

Dennis McNally (the band's official historian) wrote: "Late in May [1968], they flew to St. Louis for two nights, traveling 2000 miles to sell fewer than 400 tickets. The promoter, of course, lost his shirt" (McNally, 2002, p.264). Despite the small crowd and lost revenue, the band played great and boy, did I have fun! "*The bus came by*," for me at least.

From some unmemorable source, LSD capsules were available for sale for a couple of bucks. The acid was reported to be an Owsley product (the underground chemist later famous for his manufacture of high grade LSD). But, no one ever knew anything about the true quality of that or any black market drug. I swallowed a capsule with little hesitation and sat down on the concrete floor of the armory to await the acid trip. This was my first experience with LSD. It seemed most of the other people at the concert had similarly indulged.

A big spinning mirrorball (only later called a "disco ball") threw fragments of light all around the empty space. There was lots of room in the warehouse. An opening band played for a while. Later with no fanfare, the Grateful Dead came out and spread out all over a makeshift stage. Six people composed the band. The odd thing was there were two drum kits, and two drummers. All of the band were unkempt long hairs. They wore paisley, polka dot, and striped clothes—and looked bizarre even for that time. But, when the concert started, they became musical workmen. The band had apparently had been doing this kind of gig for several years.

In 1968 the Grateful Dead made a breakthrough in how they approached their craft. A strong jazz element had entered the music. Much of their sound was a marriage of rock instruments with jazz techniques, soaked in acid. The whole idea of a suite of songs linked together by improvised "jams," or dissolving into a period of "space" or free noise, was foreign to rock (which was dominated by the 3.5 minute A.M. radio-friendly format), but natural in the jazz world. The band also borrowed from classical music and played shows symphonically, as a series of movements between "segues" in which various songs could flow together without stopping. At the start of '68, they embraced the idea of "segueing" everything. The symbol ">" has technical meaning in Grateful Dead music. It stands for a segue into the next tune without interruption. An early setlist in 68 from a Grateful Dead archive speaks for itself.

"Dark Star> China Cat Sunflower> The Eleven> Feedback; New Potato Caboose> Born Cross-Eyed> Feedback> Spanish Jam; Cryptical Envelopment> The Other One> Cryptical Envelopment> Good Morning Little School Girl"[4]

In concert, they would play non-stop for hours, flowing from one tune to the next, only occasionally constrained by the structure of their song. Then, they would take a break and do it some more. Their concerts often lasted four hours or more. I learned later one always got their money's worth at a Grateful Dead concert!

In many of their songs, they would play long instrumental runs filled with many notes from their prolific guitar player, Jerry Garcia. He didn't play traditional guitar "lead" solos. Instead, his guitar went almost non-stop throughout a tune like a bouncing ball from *Sing Along With Mitch* (a corny musical TV show of the era). The notes from the guitar bubbled up and down in rapid succession. Their music and the LSD gave me synesthesia, i.e. I could see sound! His notes were visibly animated on a imaginary music staff to me. Some critics would consider his guitar playing as "noodling"—almost random notes. But to my ears, the guitar was full of melody and always had a sense of direction. The music sounded complex and dense at times. A blast of sound would erupt from many instruments, guitars, bass, organ, and drums. During this jam, all of the instruments would do different takes on the melody of the song, all at the same time. Each instrument played independent of the other, but somehow they were all in sync. This simultaneous soloing is one of the many things the Grateful Dead introduced to rock music.[5] Their vocals have always been considered weak. Admittedly, none of the band members could sing very well. But, their vocals were always *"ragged but right"* and had a strong element of masculinity and soul.

But that night, I was bewildered by this new sound. I wasn't familiar with their music and everything sounded strange and other-worldly to me. I'm sure it had something to do with the LSD I'd ingested an hour before. It was a pleasant strange, however. The band was clearly enjoying making their music and the vibes between the band and the audience were very good. There was no posturing or stagemanship (except for

Grateful Dead St. Louis Armory May 1968. ©Tom Tussey tusseyphoto.com

Pigpen who was a charismatic frontman). Apparently, the Grateful Dead was aware they were creating a new form of music. To make it even stranger, the Grateful Dead was the first band I knew of which used two drummers. Two guys banged away on separate drum kits in unison at the back of the stage. The sight of those two synchronized guys playing ratta-tat-tat-ratta-ratta-tat-tat-ting-ting-ting-ratta-tat-tat on the drums made me think I was hallucinating and seeing double. Of course they also generated twice the power of most percussionists. But, there were tremendous dynamics to their sound. Unlike most rock bands, they didn't always play at full volume. They could sound like a steam engine rolling down the tracks. But, the music would sometimes lower its volume and sound delicate—punctuated with droning gongs, bells, and twinkling chimes. However, I also heard sounds within their music, which sometimes sounded cartoon-like and goofy. This was the Grateful Dead and me on acid in 1968 at the Armory in St. Louis.

The band was at the height of its psychedelic musical experimentation. Their record in 1968 was *Anthem of the Sun*, their second album. That night they sang weird songs from it like "Cryptical Envelopment." Some of the lyrics are as follows:

"The summer sun looked down on him / his mother could but frown on him /
And all the others sound on him / but it doesn't seem to matter /

*And when the day had ended / with rainbow colors blended /
His mind remained unbended / he had to die / you know he had
to die"*
--excerpt from "Cryptical Envelopment"

These were kind of grim lyrics and completely unfamiliar to me.
But, somehow the song made a bit of sense as part of my own
psychedelic experience. Maybe it was the end of my old *Archie
and Jughead* teenage self? I imagined my new acid-fueled
essence was exchanging energy with all the busy molecules
around me. That evening, although thoroughly dumbfounded,
I experienced just a flash of something I considered mysterious
and supernatural with the Grateful Dead. And...it was a hell
of a lot of fun! Their music was intentionally shaped by this
experience.

I had no idea at the time, but the Grateful Dead had been
the "houseband" of the Acid Tests in California, before LSD
became illegal. Ken Kesey and the Merry Pranksters, threw
wild public parties on the West coast with fifty gallon drums of
kool-aid spiked with LSD during 1965-66. The Grateful Dead
had honed both their sound and their concert experience at
these crazy events. Thus, they were literally the soundtrack
for many, many psychedelic trips. Although the law put an end
to the public guzzling of electric kool-aid, the Grateful Dead
continued doing essentially the same thing underground.[6] The

Acid Tests formed the concert template the band used for their entire career (Trager, 1997, p. 6). That night at the Armory was certainly an Acid Test for me, my friends, and couple of hundred other folks.

But, the Grateful Dead chaffed at the idea of being a psychedelic band. Garcia insisted the band simply played dance music, "*We still feel that our function is as a dance band...We like to play with dancers....nothing improves your time like having somebody dance. It pulls the whole thing together, and it's also a nice little feedback thing*" (Jackson, 1999, p.109). He described the Dead's long jams as being useful to play to roomfuls of zonked-out dancers who'd lost all concept of time.

"*When you're playing for people who are dancing and getting high, you can dance easy to a half-hour tune and you can even wonder why it ended so soon*" (Ibid, p. 123).

I saw scattered throughout the sparse audience in the Armory couples flailing about wildly in uninhibited ecstatic movement. It was the first time I witnessed freeform "space dancing." There was movement—gyration, swaying, spinning, and waving hands everywhere. The Grateful Dead's concerts were never all about the band. The audience was as much a part of the concert as the band. As the band played harder and faster, the more the audience responded. This relationship with the audience was unknown to me. It was completely different from any prior rock concert I attended. As Garcia stated earlier, I witnessed the audience form a reciprocal relationship—a wonderful circuit of energy—with the band as they played. It appeared that actual sparks were flying everywhere between the audience and band.

During the concert in St. Louis, Jerry Garcia was animated on stage and played the role of Captain Trips, at least for me. It seemed, he often picked a person out in the audience, made eye contact, bounced his head to his notes from his guitar and entrained a member of the audience (in this case—me) in the movement. It was kind of like being dribbled up and down as a basketball. Maybe it was my heightened imagination on acid. I spent most of that evening clinging to the concrete floor while my head bobbed in the air to the music—completely quickened by the frenzy of his electric guitar. Some of the time, I laid on my back watching fireworks, exotic landscapes, and kaleidoscopic images behind my eyelids. The concert was a mystifying musical environment of swirling sounds and colors, swimming in musical notes—synesthesia actualized.

I was astounded by the Dead in concert and became an instant devotee. Remember I had already seen some famous bands play. The Grateful Dead was not my first concert rodeo. Today, I have no doubt this experience was not for everyone. You either liked the Grateful Dead, or you didn't. Their concerts were an active romp not geared for the passive consumer. In retrospect, it is my contention the innovative music of the Grateful Dead was extremely important at that time. They left an indelible mark on modern music and culture. The sounds, the audience, the atmosphere, and of course the drugs, made a Grateful Dead concert utterly unique.

At almost a cellular level, the music of the Grateful Dead became embedded in my sinew and bones that night in St. Louis *1*-2-3-4-*2*-2-3-4-*3*-2-3-4 (12/8 time). Those heavy drum beats are in my marrow. That night at the Armory, "*the bus came by and I got on*" for a trip to never-ever land.

Later that evening, going home while still high, my body was all distorted. As I placed my foot on the floorboard of my ride home, the distance to the car's floor felt like 20 feet, my leg like an elastic rubber band. Thank God I made it home safely. I had survived a modern rite of passage, my personal hero's journey, and had been completely transformed by the Grateful Dead experience. I was certainly "*on the bus*" and my life-long strange trip had begun.

Chapter 2

*"Let it be known there is a fountain /
that was not made by the hands of
men"*

From "Ripple" 1970
by Robert Hunter and Jerry Garcia

Grateful Dead concerts provided an opportunity to
transcend the humdrum banality of everyday life and to access
a sacred reality for many Dead Heads. Even in the beginning
of his career Jerry Garcia sensed his band was on to something
way outside the bounds of the cultural upheaval of the day. He
stated, *"For me, the lame part of the Sixties was the political
part, the social part. The real part was the spiritual part."*[1] The
Grateful Dead was intentionally plugged into that spiritual part,
resulting in many Dead Heads believing a Grateful Dead concert
was a semi-religious experience. Although free from dogmatic

beliefs, a Dead concert could be described as "church." Phil Lesh confirmed,

> "every place we play is church. And what is church, really? It's a place where people come together to get outside themselves and deal with something bigger. In our case, it's not us that they're dealing with that's bigger than them, it's the totality of the combination of us and them – that community, that actual spiritual oneness in the moment." [2]

These concerts were a place where one could be connected with positive energy, ritual, fellowship, love, and fun. One could sense "we are all one" at almost a molecular level. Psychedelic drugs certainly played a role facilitating such experiences since the early acid tests in the mid-'60s. But most would argue these drugs were merely optional tools and not the extraordinary experience itself. It is evident this spiritual makeup of the band's appeal made the Grateful Dead exceptional in the world of popular musical entertainment throughout their entire career.

After my first encounter with the band in 68, I had a formidable spiritual experience at another Grateful Dead concert two years later. In 1970, the Grateful Dead blew my mind at Mammoth Gardens (currently the Fillmore) in Denver. I know writing about events like this is an almost futile task. But, to dispel any thought that this is only my hyperbole, I include a newspaper review, which reinforces my evaluation of the special night. The concert reviewer stated,

> *"Magic is alive and well. It exists in the form of one of the few truly unique bands rock has produced, the Grateful Dead,...The Grateful Dead produce music on a level that most groups don't even know exist. The songs themselves are only frameworks, only foundations on which the Dead build their dazzling multi-layered skyscrapers of sound....a breath-taking explosion of unified talent"* (*Colorado Springs Sun*, April 30, 1970, unknown page).[3]

That night, during one of their majestic musical crescendos, I remember having a distinct ecstatic vision of a burning Aztec sunrise. While doing the hippie shuffle (dancing?) in the audience with friends, my chest was filled with radiance from zigzag rays of hot colored light which emanated from a huge sun ball of pulsating energy. Solar flares enveloped my heart chakra. In my upper torso, the sun's corona appeared to glow like molten plasma. These visions were coupled with a great emotional expansion within me. A sense of "oneness" with everything and everyone gave me the impression a veil had been lifted temporarily from my consciousness. I was not alone—but instead united in harmony with the universe itself.

My words don't capture the event. It was INEFFABLE—beyond verbal description—a well recognized characteristic of a valid mystical experience (James, 1902, p. 286). To say it was a mountain top experience for me is an understatement and I have never experienced anything exactly like it again. Yet hoping to recreate it, I have chased that magic moment many times. That intense vision has helped inform my artistic and spiritual life since.

A very ecstatic experience!

I wonder how many other people had similar experiences at Grateful Dead concerts. I assume few ever went to a Lady Gaga, Rolling Stones, Jay-Z, Taylor Swift, etc., etc. concert and had a similar experience. Maybe I'm wrong? But, I know there were many thousands who had similar incidents with the Grateful Dead. The band was notorious for changing lives. The spiritual impact of the band has been well documented elsewhere. Dead Heads widely reported mystical experiences, which shared three common characteristics; ineffable, euphoric, and unified with others (Adams and Sardiello, 2000, p. 115). Some have even reported encounters with distinct supernatural entities associated with Grateful Dead performances (Sylvan, 2002, p. 97).

A few months later when I heard the song "Ripple" for the first time, I was a 19 year old aimless sophomore at the University of Colorado in Boulder. The song's spiritual message from my acid test heroes immediately intrigued me. At that time, Boulder was one of several epicenters of the counter-culture in the USA. It was a wild time both to be a young man and to be at that particular school. In 1970, the hippie-dippy idealism of the '60s came crashing down on bell-bottomed believers like me.

Altamont, billed as "Woodstock West" outside of San Francisco, had capped off December, 1969 in an ugly disaster. While Woodstock represented peace and love, Altamont characterized conflict and violence. The event was immediately viewed as the end of the hippie era and the finale of late-1960s American youth culture. As a member of that tribe, the repercussions from that event and others were unsettling. My generation's idealism imploded at Altamont. The vision of a harmonic unicorn and rainbow society, which would overturn the dreary establishment of my parents, was dashed.

Just a few months later, my university shut down. In May, 1970 the school was on strike due to the expansion of the Vietnam war into Cambodia and the Kent State massacre. Welcome to my college life. Rah rah rah, sis boom bah—go team! Innocent college high jinks of the past like goldfish eating and phone booth jamming had been replaced by the Students for a Democratic Society (SDS) and the Manson family.

Simultaneously, even the Beatles broke up. John Lennon who originally wanted to hold our hand, now sang "*I don't believe in Beatles. I just believe in me, Yoko and me, and that's reality.*"[7] Something profound had ended for my generation. It is hard to imagine the turbulence of that time in retrospect. Past history felt irrelevant and had no bearing on an uncertain future without the Fab Four to lead the way.

I was also in personal transition—leaving adolescence, becoming a man while trying to make some sense of my place in the world. My psychedelic experiences were impossible for me to reconcile with my own disillusionment. I lacked any formal spiritual discipline or religious framework to help me integrate those profound events into my everyday life.

Later in the Fall of 1970, I remember hearing the beautiful music in the song "Ripple" on the Grateful Dead's sixth album, *American Beauty*. Since the album *Workingman's Dead*, the band had become much more song focused. The influence of other popular music of the day, like Crosby, Stills, and Nash, had encouraged the band to improve their singing. The results on *American Beauty* were astounding to my ears. They had come a long way from the free-wheeling improvisational acid-rock band of just a few short months earlier. Robert Hunter noted,

> *"It was a surprise to us–as it was to everybody else: this machine-eating, monster-psychedelic band is suddenly putting out sweet, listenable material."[8]*

The songs were short, melodic, and the vocal harmonies sounded angelic.

Blatant spiritual imagery abounds. The song speaks of "*a fountain*," "*still water*," "*harps unstrung*," full and empty "*cups*," and a "*path that is for your steps alone*." "Ripple" almost has the gist of a religious hymn. Jerry Garcia had some misgivings about singing such a sacred song. He even remarked, "*When I sing that song. I say to myself, 'Am I really a Presbyterian minister?'*" (McNally, 2002, p. 376). "Ripple" is probably in the top five songs of most Dead Heads. When asked by *Rolling Stone* to name a certain lyric of which he was particular proud, Robert Hunter responded *"Let it be known there is a fountain / That was not made by the hands of men"*.[10]

Robert Hunter ©Jay Blakesberg www.blakesberg.com

Life Lessons in their Songs

The spiritual message of the Dead was eventually reflected in other songs from their later repertoire. For example, in the song "The Wheel," Jerry sang, *"Small wheel turn by the fire and rod / Big wheel turn by the grace of god / Every time that wheel turn round / Bound to cover just a little more ground."* "Box of Rain," "Blues for Allah," "Eyes of the World," and "Eternity" all are songs with spiritual messages. The Bahamian lullaby, "We Bid You Goodnight," covered somewhat tongue-in-cheek by the band, included the surprisingly evangelical words *"I love you / but Jesus loves you the best."* God and the Devil, Cain and Abel, Abraham and Isaac, Esau, Moses, Sampson and Delilah, Gideon, and St. Stephen are among the many biblical characters appearing in their songs. The band even referred to themselves as *"Jehovah's favorite choir"* in the song "The Music Never Stopped." Many other metaphors in their lyrics regarding a relentless "fate" (*"Let fate decide the rest"*—"Built to Last"), the role of sublime "light" (*"have you seen the light?"*— "Uncle John's Band"), and the cosmic "river" (*"Listen to the river sing sweet songs / to rock my soul"*—"Broke Down Palace") also reinforced the band's unique theological underpinnings.

Their lyrics played with the archetypal journey from home (safety) to exile (chaos), and a return home (redemption)—*"If I knew the way / I would take you home"* ("Uncle John's

Band"). Home is the final destination for comfort. *"Going home, going home / by the water's side I will rest my bones"* ("Brokedown Palace"). Consequently, the Grateful Dead's musical compositions mimicked the arc of a hero's journey on a good acid trip. On LSD, intrepid psychonauts often traveled from a normal state, to a disordered one. Sometimes the peak was ecstatic. Other times it could be terrifying. After wrestling with psychic issues, eventually most trippers would return home to their new normal state. Frequently, they returned with fresh wisdom to share with their community. This odyssey roughly resembled the common path of heroes, from Hercules to Luke Skywalker, in world mythology.

Grateful Dead performances began with well-defined songs and orderly arrangements. In the second set as shows progressed, songs lengthened and segued together. Sometimes they fused into seamless layers of improvisation. Although these flights could be melodious and beautiful, the later ritual "Drums" and especially the "Space" musical interlude was often chaotic, atonal, noisy and often just downright scary. Eventually, toward the show's end in a subtle catharsis, order was restored from chaos. Wisdom was derived from the madness. Light emerged from darkness. Beauty from dissonance. Again, music would gradually take the form of coherent songs. The audience would be sonically reoriented toward home.

In concert, Dead Heads found a model of their own personal voyages, buoyed by the promise of resolution and eventual homecoming. This musical journey made Dead shows utterly unique. The music, sometimes coupled with psychoactive drugs, and reinforced by the community of Dead Heads, created a set and setting ripe for spiritual experience. Thus the community provided roots, while the music and the drugs bestowed wings.

Another extraordinary feature of a Grateful Dead performance was virtually everyone danced, even those flat-footed folks like me. For many, the dance and freedom of movement comprised an important part of their ritual. The energy which emerged from an audience of thousands where everyone danced was an incredible phenomena. This movement of energy formed a circle of feedback for the band and their fans. When it all came together a magic "X factor" happened—the same kind of zone, or altered state, of high performance athletes.

Time and space disappeared. Thoughts were suspended. Band and audience were absorbed in the creative eternal moment.

Joseph Campbell, the famous academic mythologist, was amazed that ancient worldwide myths he had documented were alive at a modern American rock and roll concert. To his surprise, he witnessed the following at a Grateful Dead show:

> "when you see 8,000 kids all going up in the air together ...Listen, this is powerful stuff ! ... This is more than music. It turns something on in here (the heart?). And what it turns on is life energy. This is Dionysus talking through these kids. ...It doesn't matter what the name of the god is, or whether it's a rock group or a clergy. It's somehow hitting that chord of realization of the unity of God in you all." [11]

Unlike any other band, the Grateful Dead understood their music was transformational. Mickey Hart famously addressed the shamanistic quality of the music. He claimed the band was not really in the entertainment business, but instead in the "*transportation business*" (McNally, 2002, p. 538). According to him, they moved minds and raised consciousness. At the intersection of Post Street and Steiner in San Francisco in 1978, Bill Graham, the famous concert promoter, posted a large billboard advertisement for a Grateful Dead concert, which read, "*They're not the best at what they do, they're the only ones who do what they do.*"

Other cultural influences coincided with the Dead's spiritual signposts in "Ripple" and pushed me onto a seeker's journey. One of my heroes and part of the Grateful Dead extended family, Ken Kesey, offered another guide to the sacred. In 1971, in *The Last Supplement to the Whole Earth Catalog*, Kesey wrote a reflection on a near-fatal auto-train collision, which almost took his son's life. The following was an unexpected endorsement from the lysergic Big Chief himself:

> *"The first tool I would like to point out, then, is the Bible. All of it. All the rest of your life. I won't list an address where to send for it. You can pick one up yourself, look in the top drawer of the next motel desk you come across if need be. It's nice to have your own, too. Get familiar with it and it's drama. Take your time. Get a purple satin bookmark and keep your place and ease through a chapter or two before you go to sleep, (it'll wipe the slate of your mind clean of Lever Brothers and you'll dream like Milton), or just cut in here and there now and then during the day, in a little quiet place with a bit of hash and some camomile tea with honey and lemon in it. A little at a time, steadfastly, and maybe a big hit once every week or so, say, for instance, on Saturday (for the Old Testament) and Sunday (for the New). Keep it up a while. You'll be amazed"* (Kesey, 1971, p. 5).

So when I heard the Grateful Dead sing about a fountain not made by the hands of men, I wanted to find out more about it. I needed to fill my cup and drink from those waters! So, I took Kesey's testimonial about the Bible to heart. If such a famous acid head said so, maybe it would be "cool" to read it for myself?

Additionally, in the early '70s, Ram Dass's seminal work, *Be Here Now,* tantalized me with tales of transcendence. His book had a major impact on the counterculture. Many eventually followed his lead into formal religious institutions, like Buddhism, Hinduism, or even orthodox Judaism, to help frame and integrate their previous experiences with psychedelics. I read Ram Dass's book and became an evangelical Christian. Go figure.

I won't go into the details of this long sojourn. But, to say my embrace of organized Christian religion fulfilled a need in my soul is an understatement. At the time, I needed stability, black and white morality and, most of all, a reason to get out of bed each morning. All of this was satisfied by my early embrace of Christianity. Like many others in the early '70s, I became a "Jesus Freak," a true believer, and a Bible thumper. Along the way, I even got a graduate degree in theology. Some years later, I found myself and my young family living in South America, speaking a foreign language, and acting as missionaries of the Good News.

Now, I must say my beliefs are different. I consider my time in the Christian church as just one step on my spiritual path. At some point along the way, I popped the cork on the bottle of organized religion. Although I consider my time there to be valuable, I believe I matured, became more self-confident, and escaped what I consider to be the confinement of the traditional Christian church.

Today, I consider myself to be spiritual. But, I do not identify with any particular religion. There is an ancient parable about blind men who encounter an elephant. One feels the beast's trunk. He proclaims an elephant is like a snake. Another feels its ear and says the elephant is akin to a fan. A third grabs hold of its leg. He assures his companions the beast is similar to a tree. Each is convinced he knows the entirety of the elephant, and his companions are completely wrong. Likewise, all religions are comparable in my opinion. They each perceive a bit of our spiritual reality, believe it is the whole truth, and reject all others' perceptions.

Today, we have all witnessed horrors in the name of fanatical religious beliefs. Murder in the name of religion is now part of the global environment, which has been broadcast on TV news. The events on 09/11/2001 should have been an alarming wake-up call for all flavors of religion that claim an exclusive grasp of the truth. Common sense should tell us assertions of religious "absolute truth" are suspect, if not outright dangerous. By the way, the Grateful Dead never intended to inspire that kind of fanaticism. The song "Ripple" declared the uniqueness of each spiritual journey as a path, which *"is for your steps alone."* Elsewhere, Hunter qualified, *"Believe it, if you need it / if you don't, just pass it on"* ("Box of Rain").

During my life, I have had only hints and glimpses of a spiritual reality, which lies beneath the surface of my day-to-day routines. I hardly claim to understand it all. The older I get, the less I know of a higher power. But at that long ago Grateful Dead concert, where I had a vision of an Aztec sun burning in my chest, I saw a spectacular topology. At that moment, I felt connected to all humanity and the universe (God?) itself. All the markings of a classic mystical experience were present. Perhaps it was a quick sip from a metaphorical *"fountain"* not made by human hands of which the song "Ripple" spoke.

> **The words of "Ripple" have inspired me throughout my spiritual journey.** ***"Let it be known there is a fountain / that was not made by the hands of men,"*** **is a proclamation I have embraced. Recognizing that reality has refreshed my parched soul many times.**

I know there are others who share similar stories like mine regarding the Grateful Dead and this sacred fountain. But, the impact of this song has been far reaching for me. Certainly, it has helped me through some difficult times. I have shared "Ripple" with my children as a lullaby. I have sung it around campfires. I have also played the song at the bedside of a fading hospice patient. These are important ways the golden words of this song have rippled through my life.

"There is a road no simple highway /
between the dawn and the dark of night /
And if you go no one may follow /
That path is for your steps alone"

from "Ripple"

Chapter 3

"Sometimes the light's all shining on me / other times I can barely see"

From "Truckin'" 1971
by Robert Hunter, Jerry Garcia, Bob Weir, and Phil Lesh

The song "Truckin'" appeared on the *American Beauty* record in November, 1970. In this autobiographical song, the band describes many aspects of its life on the road. (Although written by committee, I'll refer to Hunter as the main lyricist.) *"Sometimes the light's all shining on me / other times I can barely see,"* are some of the most recognizable lyrics from the Grateful Dead. These lyrics may have literally referred to the harsh spotlight, which occasionally illuminated the musicians' performance and other times left them on a dark wing of an unlit stage. But certainly, the broader meaning has to do with the ups and downs experienced on the band's journey.

These words have provided guide posts for me along my personal path. They have helped me remember that life is not always an ecstatic joy ride. Sometimes there are unpleasant times. Hardships are to be expected. Whatever the dichotomy, light or dark, happy or sad, roses or thorns, both aspects are part of the human experience. This has been one of the most significant lessons I've learned from the Grateful Dead.

The band had experienced five years of life on the road when these words were first written. A number of peaks and valleys were already etched in their careers. From the beginning, they were a much adored San Francisco band. But, drug casualties ("*Sweet Jane*"), police busts ("*Bourbon Street*"), and general hassles from the establishment ("*they just won't let you be..Oh no!*"), were part of the downside to being young musicians. The song makes clear these counter-cultural cowboys were not late 20th century pampered rock stars. At that time in their careers, they had no bubbles or insulation to shield their problems. The band was especially vulnerable to run-ins with the cops regarding marijuana and other drugs like their fans. In fact, the audience's identification with the band as "just like us" was one of the factors in the band's early mystique and popularity.

I am a first generation Dead Head, I am also a baby boomer. As such, my parents were part of a generation, which experienced the Great Depression and World War II. Their lives had been marked with the hardships and uncertainty from both major historic events. My dad was a Marine who fought at Iwo Jima and later walked through the rubble of Hiroshima. He had witnessed a lifetime worth of horrors at a young age. My mother was raised in a hand-to-mouth fashion by a widowed mom who paid the bills by washing and ironing other peoples' clothes. My mom worked her way through high school, went to college, became a nurse, and escaped a life of small town poverty. Both parents experienced other drama, including loss of siblings and other loved ones. Like many people of their generation, my own folks didn't talk much about their challenges. Quiet acceptance of both the joys and despair of their lives was the norm for them and their stoic peers. Tom Brokaw observed regarding my parents' great generation, "*They were proud of what they accomplished but rarely discussed their experiences, even with each other*" (Brokaw, 1998, p. 15).

I was fortunate to have loving parents. Perhaps out of their natural desire to shield us offspring from life's problems or as a result of Dr. Spock's "child-centered" approach to parenting, my folks kept the many problems they encountered from my brother and me when we were kids. For example, my grandmother's death from cancer was a hushed affair. No one could discuss a betrayal from my father's business partners. My aunt's hospitalization due to depression was a censored family topic. I am quite sure all this silence sprang from the best intentions of my folks. There are many other examples, but the

result was the same. My parents tried to safeguard us kids and expose us only to the best and most positive experiences in our childhood. That was reasonable and loving on their part. Some would probably say I was a spoiled American middle-class white kid because of my *Leave it To Beaver* upbringing. I am appreciative of the support and privilege my family provided and don't blame anyone else for any of my resulting foibles. And...I probably made the same mistakes with my kids.

> **But somehow, I got the impression, at an early age, that life was supposed to be untroubled. I didn't have much experience seeing my elders deal with their personal problems. Therefore, I believed life was supposed to be tidy— happy, comfortable, and content.**

I am quite sure many others have shared this rosy illusion in their adolescence. It may even be a trait of immaturity. Coming out of my teens, when I first started meeting problems on my own, I thought this was abnormal. Issues with friends, girls, drugs, the Vietnam war, college, jobs, career, faith, purpose, etc... were difficult and confusing. (Other generations may have their own issues.) Why was it so hard for me to have a clear uncluttered path through these obstacles? It was almost overwhelming.

Each day was full of insurmountable problems, for me. A trivial car repair could throw me off course. Because I was distressed by these things I thought, "*There must be something terribly wrong with me!*" I became depressed, somewhat isolated and sought out professional counseling for the first time in my life because of my perceived abnormal condition. Going to a shrink at that time reinforced my neurosis. I felt like a sicko—damaged goods.

With more time, a little maturity and the influence of others, including the Grateful Dead, I began to gradually see life has its moments of both light and darkness.

> **As an adult, I came to recognize that our odyssey was not one joyful delirious experience after another. *"Sometimes the light's all shinning on me / other times I can barely see,"* expresses a more balanced and realistic view.**

Robert Hunter's words have helped me appreciate and articulate the turbulence of my own path. Like many others, I've had great joys—friends, family, kids, love, passion, spiritual experiences, and some degree of career success. I've also been through great disappointments—heartbreak, divorce, failure, and death of loved ones. I now consider these incidents to be a normal part of the ebb and flow of my time while spinning on this planet. No one can escape the ups and downs of our living journey. In one moment, a person is flying high. The next moment can bring anxiety, fear, or some horrible incident. It happens to us all and is part of the innate nature of human existence.

"Sometimes the light's all shining on me / other times I can barely see."

We face these challenges constantly in every area of our lives. During the course of any day, I am confronted with mundane entanglements like traffic jams and leaky water pipes. These hassles can be aggravating and ruin my otherwise good day. Sometimes, I confess, I still lose my temper and cuss the universe while broken pipes drip water on my kitchen floor. Larger issues such as health crises, money worries or relationships problems can still overwhelm me. But, most people have a hard time accepting and dealing with these kinds of challenges. I have been one. Some of us run away from problems because we don't want to accept reality the way it is. The fact is we all have to deal with difficult problems throughout our lives, whether in one's personal life or career. Many self-help books are full of varying tips and remedies for negotiating our dark issues. I will spare any bromides here. But, it has helped me to remember, "*Sometimes the light's all shining on me / other times I can barely see.*" That little ditty smacks of a cosmic truth.

Robert Hunter expressed another slant on the idea of life's inherent turbulence in other Grateful Dead songs. In "Uncle John's Band," he wrote "*Cause when life looks like easy street / there is danger at your door.*" These words warn us to consider our horizons with a degree of humility, if not outright apprehension. Especially, those most comfortable on "*easy street,*" should beware they may be blindsided by changing fortunes. Our culture is full of examples of triumph to tragedy stories from *Hamlet* to *Easy Rider* and *Scarface*. America loves to build up celebrities, only to see them torn down later. Richard Nixon, O.J. Simpson, Anthony Weiner, Lance Armstrong, Matt Lauer, Bill Cosby, Harvey Weinstein, Jeffery Epstein, Sam Bankman-Fried, are just a few examples of those who basked in the bright spotlight of public approval only temporarily. All of these dishonored souls would undoubtedly now concur, *"Sometimes the light's all shining on me / other times I can barely see."* There appears to be a universal application of this principle, regardless of one's station in life.

A very conscientious friend of mine expressed a similar idea with more colorful language when her blinding jealousy came to light. She had envied a couple who appeared to have everything. They were on *"easy street,"* while my friend struggled with her supposedly inferior circumstances. To her, they were the perfect family, with 2.5 ideal children—all with straight teeth, a lovable obedient dog, and an eco-friendly white picket fence. When the coveted couple split up in an acrimonious divorce, my friend was dumbstruck. She learned her lesson and shared her new insight with me that, *"there's shit on everyone's doorstep."* I've always considered her epiphany to be a Zen-like proverb—one I've valued enough to repeat many times. Although we sometimes think we are the only ones with troubles, it is just a common human delusion. In accord with the bard's lyrics all of us, even those I've placed on bright pedestals, spend some time in the dark.

It is not surprising there is a parallel between the band's message here and a great deal of sacred tradition. Even the

Bible speaks of life's roller coaster ride, "*To everything there is a season, a time for every purpose under heaven:...a time to weep, a time to laugh, a time to mourn, and a time to dance*" (Eccles. 3:1-4). Most Dead Heads can easily embrace "*a time to dance.*" It's much harder to accept a "*time to mourn.*"

Jack Kornfield a popular American Buddhist, psychologist, and author wrote an entire book on the duality of light and darkness in our lives. According to Kornfield, in mysterious ways the heart is like a flower, which opens and closes again and again in each cycle from daylight to nighttime. This is our nature. The only astonishing thing is how unexpected this truth can be.

Even for Dead Heads, it is as if deep down we all hope some experience, some great "high," one more profound psychedelic trip, another euphoric concert, an enraptured sexual experience, or even enough years of dedicated practice via yoga, meditation, or maybe even mountain climbing, might finally lift us beyond the mundane struggles of the world. We cling to some hope we can finally rise above the wounds of our human pain, never to have to suffer them again. But, if you get high, eventually you can gently land back on earth on your feet—or crash down in a big heap. Kornfield wrote "*We all know that after the honeymoon comes the marriage, after the election* comes the hard task of governance. In spiritual life it is the same: After the ecstasy comes the laundry" (Kornfield, 2000, p. xiii). "Sometimes the light's all shining on me / other times I can barely see" is an expression of this same spiritual truth.

Ram Dass was certainly one man who has spent a lot of time in the light. He became a cultural icon for us baby boomers with the publication of Be Here Now in 1971. The handmade book was a hip chronicle of Richard Alpert's transformation into a "Servant of God," which followed getting kicked out of Harvard along with Tim Leary, launching the psychedelic movement, and meeting his guru in India.

As a spiritual celebrity from the '60s, Ram Dass lived comfortably on his lucrative speaking gigs and superstar engagements. Most of his life was spent in the warm adulation from many fellow seekers. But in 1997, while writing a book on aging, changing, and dying, he suffered a massive stroke, which left him unable to speak clearly and partially paralyzed. The loss of his glib tongue threatened his livelihood. Over night, the holy man who had spent a life time as a care giver, became handicapped, in need of twenty-four-hour care himself. His eventual embrace of the impaired condition as a gift of "fierce grace" provided an example of how so-called tragedy can enter one's life and yet be a source of many unexpected blessings.

The teaching he offered is all circumstances—daylight or darkness—can be seen as supernatural grace.[3]

Rather than merely complain as the unfortunate victim of a terrible turn of events, Ram Dass used the stroke as a means for further growth and compassion. He claimed not to have been cured of the stroke, but he had been healed by it. Besides, according to him, the stroke provided a great ending for his book pitched at us declining baby boomers.

These words from the Grateful Dead's lyrics have provided some useful guidance for my life. I no longer consider my own ups and downs to be abnormal. I can appreciate my time both in the spotlight and in the darkness. Those messy times when I can "*barely see*," seem less pathological. My need to run to a professional counselor at every bump in my road has been greatly diminished. No one can escape the seesaw of events transpiring each day.

On the same day, which I write these words, the following things have happened in my world: 1) a national tragedy occurred resulting in the loss of life of many innocent people; 2) I took my mother to her oncologist and received good news; 3.) one of my favorite rock stars unexpectedly died; and 4) I received a small surprise check in the mail. Some of these experiences made me happy. Obviously, others made me sad.

The tally sheet for just one day illustrates that light and dark, good and bad, aces and deuces, and roses and thorns are all part of the natural drama of our lives. It has been helpful to mutter the words under my breath like a mantra, "*Sometimes the light's all shining on me / other times I can barely see.*" That is clearly one of the most important lessons I've learned from the Grateful Dead.

"Most of the cats you meet on the street speak of True Love /
Most of the time they're sittin' and cryin' at home /
One of these days they know they gotta get goin' / out of the door and down to the street all alone"

from "Truckin'"

Chapter 4

"Paradise waits on the crest of a wave"

From "Help on the Way" 1975
by Robert Hunter and Jerry Garcia

Understanding improvisation has been the key to appreciating the Grateful Dead's musical performance. Even though the structured song, and song format, grew more important with time, improvisation was the central touchstone for the band. Garcia insisted, "*I don't believe that I could play without improvising on some level, That is to say that I don't plan ahead.*" He explained,

> "*I could never bring myself to actually learn something, note for note, and play it that way more than once. It's maybe deeply rooted in anti-authoritarianism. I don't know what it is. Something in my personality just won't allow me to do it.*"[1]

The phrase, "*Paradise waits on the crest of a wave*" from the song "Help On the Way" jibes with Garcia's proclivity to compose in the moment. In another song, Bob Weir invoked the same image as he described, "*playing, like a wave upon the sand*" ("Playing in the Band") on his record *Ace*. These lyrics invoke the exuberance and the tenuous nature of the Dead's extemporaneous approach to music. Accordingly, the potential for genius and great beauty always exists, but only on the swell of a precarious and fleeting moment.

on the crest of a wave!

The Grateful Dead's style of playing, while sometimes appearing chaotic, often produced a synergy greater than the sum of its parts. On their best nights, the band members' spontaneous musical interaction would spill from the stage to engage the concert crowd in an urgent and intimate conversation. This phenomena could make every performance feel different. Each witness, stoned or sober, could experience a unique historical event, never again to be exactly repeated by the band. Night after night, fans attended shows across the country searching for what some called "the X Factor," "the secret," "the sound," or "the zone." Those are all various depictions of the ultimate jam, the indispensable improvisation, when the music played the band. It was a once-in-a-lifetime moment, which could only be experienced by being present, live and in person, in communion with band and audience in that instant. This paradise on a whitecap brought chills up the spine, rapture, and even ecstasy for fans who believed themselves part of something both important and special.

Several factors pushed the band in this improvisational direction. Two musicians, Scotty Stoneman and John Coltrane, have been recognized for teaching the band how to improvise. Stoneman was a jaw-dropping, alcoholic, bluegrass fiddler. He was the inspiration for the skeleton demon fiddler depicted on the album cover of *Blues for Allah*. The man must have played to save his soul. Garcia witnessed the emotional impact and transcendence of spontaneous jams from watching Stoneman. He stated, *"That's the first time I had the experience of being high, getting high from him, going away from it like 'what happened?' and just standing there clapping till my hands were sore"* (McNally, 2002, p. 91).

From John Coltrane the avaunt-garde jazz saxophonist, the Grateful Dead learned about <u>collective</u> improvisation. Rather than one artist stepping forward to solo, at times Coltrane's band all engaged in some spontaneous embellishment within each instrument's respective roles. As a result, with unspoken musical gestures Jerry, Bobby, and Phil evolved a technique where each instrument played a running line all the time, backed by powerful double drum percussion. Frequently, the keyboard player in the Dead was the only guy who was nailing down the basic tune while Garcia and others wove a stream of melodic notes around it. The end result was extremely fluid music. Others have called this music "*electronic Dixieland,*" where one instrument plays the basic tune and the other musicians improvise in response to it.[3] This creates a more complex polyphonic sound than the straight melodies heard in most rock music. Even after listening to this music for more than 50 years, the complexity of the sound still makes my head spin when I try to really focus on each of the instruments in the sonic frenzy of a really good Grateful Dead jam.

Ample space was provided for the band's improvisation during uninterrupted passages from one song to the next. The unifying aesthetic of bridging their music from point "A" to point "B" may have been influenced by several factors. The unbroken (taped together) typewriter scroll for Kerouac's *On the Road* was celebrated by the Beat Generation. A model of uninterrupted change could have been provided by the subtle transitions of microclimates contained within the single geography of San Francisco's Golden Gate Park. Even hallucinatory visual morphing common in the psychedelic experience itself may have further spawned their fluid style. In each remarkable case, borderless change from one state to the next is continuous and nearly imperceptible.

> **Thus, the ephemeral and invisible rim between songs became a main territory for improvisation for the band. Their vision was to produce seamless non-stop musical jams, which transformed gradually and joined one song to the next.**

Here, the Dead was not entirely alone. Even in the rock world, where the Dead's type of improvisation was unique,

1967 was the breakthrough year for joining songs together on a recorded album. The Beatles were the most influential with *Sgt Pepper's Lonely Hearts Club Band,* where several songs are notoriously linked together in clever segues (a technical musical term for an uninterrupted transition from one piece of music to another), and gaps between songs are kept to a minimum.

Unlike the Beatles, these transitions became one of the Dead's trademarks and were a real innovation in the genre of live performance. Equipped with this extemporaneous skill, the Grateful Dead became the original jam band, especially in their second set, when the band was warmed up with all the moving pieces well-oiled. Certain segues became so familiar, like blending "China Cat Sunflower" into "I Know You Riders," they appeared to some fans as just one song, but with two distinct parts.

Tapers of the Dead's music quickly took notice of these bridges between songs and accordingly began to denote segues with the symbol of the arrow ">" in their setlist documentation. Thus, the song discussed here was usually part of the sequence, which traditionally is described in the following way—"Help On the Way">"Slipknot">"Franklin's Tower." Concert recordings of multiple versions of this triplet of tunes in my own library range from fourteen minutes to twenty-four minutes in length. Although the band did improvise within the verse chorus structure of their songs, most of the difference in time is taken up by jams in the space between the songs.

To me, the ">" is really where the action was in a concert. Phil Lesh used the recurring themes of islands and open ocean to describe the segue between songs in their performance.[4] Like islands in the sea, Grateful Dead songs were steady underfoot, safe harbors, according to the bassist. But, the uncharted sea was the wild and dangerous space in between those little plots of land. Away from terra firma, out in the briny deep is where improvisation lived. In that space between songs (">") there was no map to follow or rules to guide. Practice, skill, guts, and good luck were needed to navigate that unexplored expanse. It was risky to venture into the unfamiliar deep waters of improvisation—beyond this place, there be dragons! Failure was always a close possibility. But according to Lesh, the perilous voyage could also often yield great musical treasure.

Undoubtedly the most important factor which fostered improvisation in their music was LSD. For the band, the psychedelic experience coalesced the members into a group of intuitive artists who were able to spontaneously riff off each other's idiosyncrasies while improvising over, under, and around each other in the musical moment. Lesh stated the following regarding the impact of the psychedelic on the band:

> *"What it did was, fuse our minds together in a kind of telepathic manner that allowed us to — see the best part about making our kind of music is when the music is pretty much playing us and there's no one there at all moving the fingers. That is to say we all subassume our identity in a sense in a greater whole. We call that — the group mind. That's the tool that we use to open the valve to that pipeline which funnels that greater music down through us. Stravinsky once said I am the vessel through which the music passes. In the case of the Grateful Dead, that's also the case,"* (Carlson, 2005).

Throughout the band's career, the early acid tests were "*a prototype to our whole basic trip*," Jerry Garcia told the *Rolling Stone* magazine in 1972.[6] The long hypnotic improvisational jams, the subtle sonic blur from one song to the next, the ecstatic swell of their music, the entire framework of their performance—from musical structure to chaos returning back to structure—were all artistic representations of various aspects of the psychedelic experience. Even the unique symbiosis of the Dead with their audience was enhanced by a wink and a nod to a shared psychedelic experience. Band and audience were companions on a ecstatic odyssey—and what a long strange trip it's been.

Dead Heads were always considered to be part of the band's brilliance and a mysterious ingredient in their musical performance, "*Everybody's playing in the heart of gold band*" ("Scarlet Begonias"). Good feedback from the audience, usually in the form of dancing, inspired the band members to play better, take more chances, and push their musical envelop further. Regarding the band's relationship to dancers, Phil Lesh witnessed the enormous difference audience energy could bring to a Grateful Dead concert.

"*Well, we started out playing for dancers in the ballrooms of San Francisco in the late 1960's. And that's really what we've always thought of ourselves as, as a — essentially a dance band,...they send us energy back. And so that was the main reason we played music was to get that communion going and that sense of community*" (Carlson, 2005).

One of the main reasons most of the band's studio albums were so lackluster— they missed the secret sauce created by their audience tripping the light fantastic (i.e. dancing).

Grateful Dead music never pleased everyone. Many could never appreciate the jazzy improvisational nature of this music. To critics, Garcia's guitar work sounded like overindulgent noodling, double drums reminded them of tennis shoes randomly bouncing in a household dryer, and the extended treatment of their songs was unnecessarily long and boring. Some just could not embrace a band, which required an attention span greater than three minutes, the format for most pop songs on the radio. *"Our audience is like people who like licorice,"* Jerry Garcia famously said. *"Not everybody likes licorice, but the people who like licorice really like licorice."*[7] Count me in. I really like licorice!

Criticism did not paralyze the Grateful Dead from following their unique muse. I admit due to their willingness to take chances and embrace spontaneity, they did make more mistakes than many other bands. Garcia even supposedly said, *"You go diving for pearls every night but sometimes you end up with clams"* (Scott and Halligan, 2010, p. 38) . If you hear four or five shows, one of them might be a real stinker. Sometimes they just messed up, flubbed cues, forgot lyrics, sang off key, lacked energy, or didn't even appear to listen to each other. Dead Heads were amazingly forgiving of these foibles and supported the band's intent a lot more than their results. Even in weak shows, there were often high points. Fortunately, it was also common for a bad Grateful Dead concert to be followed by a truly magnificent one.

Improvisation does not simply mean doing something without adequate preparation. Without paying the necessary dues, "winging it" can become self deluded fakery. For instance, I am not an acrobat. If I had to cross the Grand Canyon on a tightrope, it would not be improvisation, it would be suicide. I would lack the necessary practice and skill to survive. Certainly, musical improvisation requires a high degree of expertise and preparation. Like abstract painting, one should first learn to paint realistically before taking big liberties with the brush. Improvisation usually comes from time and effort spent in learning and rehearsing. Only after a technique is acquired can one make the ad-lib look so darn easy. In their early history, the Dead honed their skill by playing in private parties, pizza parlors, strip joints, and obscure venues (like the first one I attended with just a few fans in attendance at the St. Louis Armory). Continuing with a fifty-year history of the band, I believe the Grateful Dead paid the necessary price tag to improvise without a net.

Many times when the band played, their next musical choice was decided in that unique moment. That is the essence of improvisation. Today, that same technique has become more celebrated in the workplace and in life. There is hardly a facet of modern life which does not require our own improvisation. Raise a child, navigate a career, drive a car, prepare a meal— all of life requires making it up as we go. We live in a time-compressed world, in which the pace of change is constantly accelerating. The world is laced with risks of increasing turbulence, uncertainty and volatility. Today's business world is more uncertain than ever and it certainly pays to be able to think on your feet. Disrupting old habits, embracing mistakes, maximizing flexibility, and evaluating retrospectively are some of the lessons Barry Barnes learned from the band and later advocated to the business community in his book *Everything I Know About Business I Learned from the Grateful Dead*. Even in the military, where the common emphasis is on unquestionably following orders to the letter, the Marines require more creative thinking. The motto of those troops is to "*improvise, adapt, and overcome.*"[9]

The software industry, where I spent several decades gainfully employed, once advocated strict adherence to detailed and static "waterfall" requirement documents, most often written years before the software was finished. Too often, the end result downstream from the waterfall was software, which fulfilled the aging specs, but was completely obsolete upon delivery. The tech industry and business needs flowed on under the feet of the programmers. Today, the software industry tries to be more agile and responsive to end users' real demands in their development methodologies.

Almost every line of work, which involves something more than brute strength, requires an amazing amount of creative thinking. Even the most thankless jobs are often much more difficult than perceived by myopic managers. Most jobs have some challenge. There are no instruction books, which provide step-by-step guides to many of the problems faced by those of us who have ever worked for a living. Instead, innovative action is required. As the old adage states, plumbers are not paid for just tapping on pipes. But, they make good money for knowing <u>where</u> to tap. No life or career or even plumbing job can be perfectly pre-planned. Spontaneous action is often required in order to survive both on our jobs and in our personal lives.

Improvisation in any domain may lead to a transformation of consciousness. Even without the use of LSD or other psychoactive drugs, improvisation can create its own altered state. That brain state is now beginning to be both understood and highly valued. The positive and productive feeling referred to as "the zone" or "flow" is often associated with these actions. In this mind alteration, one is fully immersed on the creative task at hand. Complete absorption and a loss of one's sense of both space and time is common. Flow states certainly did not happen only to the Grateful Dead musicians and their enlivened audience. Playing sports or video games, writing, dancing, programming software, doing yoga, surfing, welding, painting, running, and many other activities can lead others to experience this "zone."

Ram Dass described a talk he gave years ago to a group of young, hippie explorers about his far-out experiences with LSD and chemically altered consciousness. In the audience was a conservative looking older woman who was somewhat out of place from the usual space cadet attendees. Surprisingly, the woman nodded and looked as though she perfectly related to all the guru was saying. Intrigued, he asked her afterward, *"what have you done in your life that brought you into those kinds of experiences?'* She leaned forward very conspiratorially and said, *'I crochet.'"*[10] Aha! Ram Dass realized that people arrive at these altered states of consciousness through a much wider spectrum of experience than he ever imagined.

Neuroscientists have confirmed the brains of freestyle rappers, jazz musicians, and other improvisers show a similar neural signature. Their flow state is different from the ordinary consciousness. During improvisation, large swatches of the brain no longer function, causing self consciousness and associated inhibitions to be diminished.[11] During Grateful Dead concerts, this same bypass must have occurred in the brains of both band and audience, when the music played the band. Both band and audience, could be transported to a place where paradise waited on the crest of the wave.

In recent years, this creative flow has become a thriving cottage industry. There are best-selling books on the flow, seminars on how to achieve it, and entire fields of study devoted to figuring out exactly how it works. One company in Austin advertises it teaches others to claim their *"flow superpowers."* Advertising materials state their staff members will coach and consult with individuals and organizations to harness this power so they can achieve peak performance.[12] For some business people, the flow state is the latest tactic for an edge on the competition. Apparently it is worth investing big chunks of cash in this newly discovered tool. On the other hand, Buddhists, artists, athletes, and particularly musicians, like the members of the Grateful Dead, have known about creative flow for ages–not to mention how to get there for much cheaper.

Not surprisingly, theatrical improvisation (improv) is actually prescribed today as a life enhancing experience. Improv is now marketed to all, not just thespians, as a near cure-all for developing the courage to step into the unknown and bypass one's fears on the metaphorical stage of life. Theaters, comedy clubs, adult education programs, and colleges are likely locales to offer popular corporate improv workshops and classes to all comers.

Increasingly, professionals in a wide range of industries are getting in on the act, finding improv to be a valuable skill to promote better listening and the ability to think on one's feet.[13] This type of improvisation is a form of live theater in which the plot, characters, and dialogue of a scene are made up in the spontaneous moment. Students come from all walks of life to take classes and learn skills in this form of creative expression. They say it offers a framework, which helps stop the "inner critic" and teaches many to find and trust their most creative and authentic self. These improvisational skills turn out to be particularly useful in jobs demanding a high degree of adaptability, which includes most of today's workforce.

The Grateful Dead surely is not responsible for all this current cultural hoop-la regarding improvisation, although they may have had some impact. They did originate a whole new genre of rock music based upon that practice. For me at least, they made improvisation really cool. This recognition of the utility, power, and value of improvisation is one of the most important lessons I've learned from the Grateful Dead.

> **Many times I have been conscious of novel circumstances that have forced me to act in some unpredictable and unplanned way. I have said to myself, *"It's a Grateful Dead thing,"* as I've taken risks, tried new things, and stepped outside of my own comfort zone.**

Even writing this book is an exercise in improvisation for me. Hopefully all these words and concepts have never been written before in exactly this way. It has been a creative endeavor for me.

In our everyday lives we are always spontaneously reacting to unpredictable and challenging circumstances. Despite the ubiquity of good intentions, strategic plans, scripts, etc., all the effort we put into what happens next is never a done deal. As Mike Tyson so eloquently stated, *"Everyone has a plan until they get punched in the mouth."* Without improvisation, we are only copying old and predictable patterns, which make us even more vulnerable to life's real knock out punches. With improvisation, the possibilities are brighter. If we trust our own ability to improvise, paradise may await us in the next ephemeral moment.

Chapter 5

"Once in a while you get shown the light / in the strangest of places if you look at it right"

From "Scarlet Begonias" 1974
By Robert Hunter and Jerry Garcia

The lyrics above come from the Grateful Dead's song

"Scarlet Begonias." It first appears on the 1974 album *From*

the Mars Hotel. This song is considered one of Hunter's and

Garcia's very best. "Scarlet Begonias" showcases Robert

Hunter at the height of his songwriting chops, pairing perfectly

with a similar achievement from Garcia's voice and guitar.[1] It

has an intricate herky-jerky rhythm and a bright memorable

melody. Few songs in the Dead repertoire can strike us in so

many ways. "Scarlet Begonias" enabled many to see their lives

from different angles while simultaneously launching them into a

hip-shaking dance groove. Cosmic truths spill from the song.

Jerry Garcia ©Chris Stone gratefulphoto.com

The lyricist's verse, "*Once in a while you get shown the light /
in the strangest of places if you look at it right,*" is one of those
Grateful Dead golden nuggets of wisdom. That poignant prose
is worthy for adorning everything from bumper stickers to granite
memorials. This phrase describes the likelihood, the improbable

setting, and the discernment necessary for obtaining uncanny insight.

Light is a form of energy, which dispels darkness and makes visible the unseen. It is one of the necessary ingredients for life itself. It is also one of the most universal symbols in art and literature. Darkness and light represent two opposing forces of nature. Good and evil, knowledge and ignorance, happiness and despair, love and hate, even life and death are all represented by the dichotomies of light and dark.

The importance of light to human history can hardly be over stated. Fire and light inflamed the torch, which cave dwellers used to drive off predatory beasts. Light has played a major role in world religions. From the first book of the Bible's divine proclamation of "*Let there be light*" (Genesis 1:3) to the Buddhist's doctrine of "*enlightenment*," the brilliance of illumination has been a desirable focus for the faithful. Today despite the archaic technology, knowledge and wisdom are still represented by a bright oil lamp. An overhead light bulb represents a smart idea.

Robert Hunter used the symbol of light in many Grateful Dead songs. A few references to light in the band's lyrics include: "*Sometimes the light's all shining on me*" ("Truckin"), "*Sunlight splatters dawn with answers*" ("St. Stephen"), "*Full of tastes no tongue can know / and lights no eye can see"* ("Attics of My Life"), and "*His job is to shed light / and not to master"* ("Lady with a Fan"). Although there are different shades of meaning, consciousness, insight, and wisdom are synonyms for the light of which Hunter speaks. This kind of knowledge has little to do with academia, grades, or book learning. It is subjective personal knowledge. One person's insight may be meaningless to everyone else on earth. Many spiritual practices are founded upon this state of illumination. Some of those practitioners actually describe themselves as "*lightworkers.*" Others who use mind expanding drugs, are often seekers of the same kind of enlightenment.

Most of us stumble along in life's dim twilight. Our drama consists of one bruise after another as we collide with random obstacles in the dark. But, once in a while we have moments of insight, understanding and grace. Those moments are ephemeral, but they somehow do make life more worth living. Those sporadic sparks certainly give me a sense my life has some meaning and purpose.

The Grateful Dead relished the idea of obscure messages and hidden meaning, which required some effort from their fans. On two of their records, the Dead's graphic artists intentionally used ambigrams in their album cover art.

An ambigram is an art form with elements having different meanings when viewed from a different direction, perspective, or orientation. On a third album, the band hid a shocking message, similar to the exaggerated image below, requiring some physical gymnastics to correctly decipher.

On the front of the Dead's third studio album Aoxomoxoa, the artist Rick Griffin created large flowing capital letters spelling out, "*GRATEFUL DEAD*." Those letters can also be read as we or I (or somebody?) clearly "*ATE THE ACID*." This provocative message must have evaded the record company execs and morality censors of the late '60s. Bill (the drummer) Kreutzmann stated, regarding the credibility and visibility of the LSD confession, "*which, I suppose, is true enough, if you look at it just right. Was that intentional? I'm not telling*" (Kreutzmann, 2015, p. 114). Also, the title wording on their sixth album, *American Beauty*, can be interpreted as *American Reality*. That was an especially remarkable album name. With both readings of the same album name, there is a juxtaposition between an idealistic America and the more nitty-gritty ugly one. The music of the band incorporated both aspects of our national character. (Listen to upbeat hippie anthem, "The Golden Road to Unlimited Devotion," along with the down and out tale of the panhandler in "Wharf Rat.")

During the 1970s, given all of the negative publicity of backward Satanic messages hidden in rock music, it is amazing the Grateful Dead actually did have a backwards message on an album cover. Maybe that was the band's way of thumbing their nose at all the hysteria. On the very album, which contains the song under discussion, *From the Mars Hotel*, there really is a hidden graphic when held upside down in front of a mirror. When viewed properly, a cryptic hieroglyphic actually says "*UGLY RUMORS.*" (That is a long way from, "*Hail Beelzebub!*"—the kind of secret backwards messages which alarmed Christian fundamentalists at the time.) Check it out! All of these are examples of the Grateful Dead's fondness for whimsy, mystery, and self-discovery. Apparently, "*looking at it right,*" was a common thread throughout both their musical and visual art.

I consider this lyric to be an important lesson for me. It alludes to the hidden wisdom found in ambiguous or obscured circumstances. Life throws these experiences our way. All of us have had numerous circumstances, subject to multiple interpretations.

> **But, I have learned it is not those circumstances we face which define us. It is much more our <u>attitudes</u> and thus the meaning we place on those circumstances which determine our welfare.**

Two people with the exact same conditions, often react in polar opposite directions depending on their perception. I know one person for whom a knee replacement was the worst possible painful inconvenience imaginable. For another, it was two months of valuable rest and relaxation. It doesn't take too many decades on this earth to realize the exact same circumstances do often produce different reactions in our human tribe.

Light and wisdom may appear in the *"strangest of places"* including hardship and disasters. My depression-era parents instilled the old adage in me at an early age—*"I felt sorry for myself because I had no shoes, until I met a man who had no feet."* Unfortunately on the mean streets of many big cities, I've been reminded of this lesson too often. An awareness of others' conditions, worse than mine, has often been a major factor to help me to look at it *"right."*

A parable about a Chinese farmer from 2,000 years ago was popularized by the influential Eastern philosopher Alan Watts.[3] Something in this old story speaks to our times and is apropos to the importance of perception. The old parable describes a farmer who had worked his crops for many years. One day his horse ran away. Upon hearing the news, his well-intentioned neighbors came to visit. "*Such bad luck*," they said sympathetically. "*Maybe*," was all the farmer replied. The next morning the horse returned, bringing with it three other wild horses. "*How wonderful*," the neighbors then exclaimed! The old man shrugged and simply said "*maybe*" again. The following day, his son tried to ride one of the untamed horses, was thrown, and broke his leg. The neighbors again came to offer their condolences on his misfortune. "*Maybe*," was all the farmer responded for the third time. The day after, military officials came to the village to draft young men into the army. Seeing the son's leg was broken, they passed by him. The neighbors then congratulated the farmer on how well things had turned out. Nevertheless, "*maybe*" was still all the wise farmer could say.

The Taoists prefer to look at life events without judgment or interpretation. According to this religion, the true significance of events can never be fully understood when they are occurring. Each event has elements of both good and bad.

Furthermore, historical events may impact the future far beyond our personal limited vision. It's easy to understand why the ancient story of the Chinese farmer resonates now, in times too full of bad news. In short, it reminds people it's best not to get too upset or attached to each and every incident which happens to us. Even something appearing gloomy and confounding can turn out to be an opportunity, when you *"look at it right."*

Dark periods of American history may have their bright side, if you look at it with a certain perspective. When I heard tales from my parents about their childhood in the Great Depression, I was often slightly envious. Although many suffered, some learned to rely on family, friends and community in ways I've never known. Like most folks of that era, my grandparents were flat broke. Their bank had failed. For years during the depression, my grandparents lived on the gracious credit extended by the neighborhood grocer. As recipients of his generosity, my grandparents paid it forward to others. My grandmother told me she often made more food than her immediate family could eat. The dinner table was frequently shared with extended family, friends, and neighbors. Everyone was welcome. My grandmother also put out a plate for hungry strangers who sought help at their backdoor. That level of hospitality is unimaginable to me today. There was "*light*" even in some of their darkest times.

How many of us have had a situation not turn out the way we wanted, only to find out something better was in store? My own dealings with unpleasant experiences, unemployment, broken relationships, and even death of loved ones have provided opportunities to gain important insights into my own life. Sometimes these strange "*places*" are especially fertile for growth. When we are most vulnerable, broken and open, often we "*get shown the light.*" Even "bad trips" can have counter intuitive results. In one study, eighty-four percent of people who had difficult psychological struggles with hallucinogenic mushroom journeys say they benefited from the painful experience.[4]

Many people can relate to the trauma of being fired and losing a job. I am not too proud to announce I've certainly had that experience—several times. Once I was fired from a management job in a conservative university in a small town in West Texas. I had worked as the Chief Information Officer in that school for over a year. The job was a challenge and a step up the ladder to a career in information technology (IT). Yet, in confidence I told a close friend I thought I'd be happier in a more progressive big city, like Austin. Soon after, I came to work at the university one morning and found my computer account was no longer active. The plug had been pulled. I couldn't log on. That is the abrupt manner IT workers are often informed of getting sacked. I was so shocked and humiliated! It had never before happened to me. *"My life was ruined and my world had ended,"* I thought. After my dismissal, due to my desire to relocate, my friend reminded me, *"I must have some powerful angels."* But, I wasn't convinced.

In my subsequent job search, I interviewed with one big wig who told me, *"In IT management, if you haven't been fired three or four times, you aren't really doing your job."* That remark did make me feel better. After many deep breaths and some time, I was fortunate to find more technical work outside of both academia and management, in the city of Austin—the place I had previously identified as where I wanted to live. Also, I discovered I was better suited for more hands-on tech work with less apple-polishing (a polite way to say *"ass-kissing"*). Most importantly, I discovered I really wasn't comfortable managing others who were doing things I didn't fully understand. Many management-types thrive on that kind of blind delegation. That is not my trip! *"Ah ha,"* the light appeared. This insight helped shape much of the rest of my professional life.

Many consider similar experiences to be the "*best thing that ever happened to them.*" A Google search of the exact three words, "fired best thing," yields nearly 348 million results at the present. Losing a job can lead us to examine our values, skills, and new opportunities.

There are many anecdotal stories of people who see the light under similarly strange circumstances. For example, as a young man, Walt Disney worked as a cartoonist for the *Kansas City Star* newspaper. Disney was eventually fired from the newspaper because, his editor said, he "*lacked imagination and had no good ideas.*"[5] Sometime after this career catastrophe, I can only think Walt Disney was shown the light when a talking mouse named Mickey appeared in his imagination. The Walt Disney Company would eventually buy *The Kansas City Star* in 1996.

A myriad of other circumstances beyond unemployment can unexpectedly turn out well in some sense. Lots of people come through traumas with major insights. Rock bottom is a common place for many to turn their life upward. Sickness can cause people to appreciate health in a more meaningful way. Life is cherished by those who survive near-death episodes. All of these types of experiences are just some examples of the "*strangest of places*" to find wisdom, insight, and revelation.

I have earned several academic degrees. But in retrospect, I've spent far too much time on my ass, sitting at a school desk, listening to the drone of supposedly learned scholars. I do value some of that formal education. I acknowledge many doors opened for me because of it. But, most of the things I've learned of real personal value didn't come in a classroom. I'm sure that is true for most people. I've been "*shown the light*" while shoveling asphalt, driving a garbage truck, and working as a janitor. I've learned lessons from rednecks, dropouts, and some truly crazy-ass people. Many revelations have occurred during my own dark nights of the soul—an especially fertile time for growth.

Not all sources of insight come from trauma. I've also been shown the light while dancing joyously to the music of the Grateful Dead. Their concerts were frequent life affirming lightposts for me and many others. Dead shows generally had a positive atmosphere, as the band and the audience interacted with each other to create a special environment of musical celebration. A concert was a weird cross between a surreal circus and a praise-based church. It was a bright combination of whimsy and wonder. There were rules and rituals. But there was also a lot of space held for freedom of expression.

The improvisational music allowed people in this setting to have improvisational thoughts. As a result, lives were changed at Dead shows. Decisions were made and creativity was inspired. People would decide to break up a relationship, move to a different town, quit a day job, or commit to a brand new challenge. One person expressed the following regarding a personal rediscovery:

> *"For me, Grateful Dead shows would remind me of my real self, as if I'd get kind of caked and blurred by too much daily experience and I would lose the recognition of my original set of intentions for life. Then I'd go to Dead shows, and those would be stripped away by the music, by the dancing, and by psychedelics, and I would see my original face again"* (Sylvan, 2002, p. 101).

The social makeup of the fans often inspired me, as well. After being around the very diverse Dead Heads with admittedly some truly freaky folks at a concert, I always felt pretty normal and mainstream in that crowd. I comfortably fit in and was reminded I hadn't really gone off the deep end...yet. This revelation gave me a new confidence in my unconventional self, beyond the show. Becoming more comfortable in my own skin was one of the side effects I surprisingly received from a Grateful Dead performance.

The following picture is referred to as autostereogram. It is a single-image, which can be viewed with the naked eyes to reveal a stereoscopic, three-dimensional image. The principle of the autostereogram is a repetitive pattern slightly changed to allow a hidden image to be visible, if you look at it right. When the eyes are adjusted, variations in the patterns are interpreted by the viewer as differences in depth. For a couple of decades this kind of art work became common place in dorm rooms, office cubes, novelty stores in the mall, and other places needing a splash of color and intrigue. When people squint, turn their head slightly, or even focus their eyes in front of the print, once in a while, floating above the background, images of porpoises, eagles, or other surprising objects may appear. I have spent a good deal of time scratching my head, trying to figure out what exactly was hidden in this kind of wallpaper. Admittedly, I am not very good at it. Often I have a hard time

seeing what others perceive more clearly with this kind of picture. Maybe this shortcoming has a broader message for me.

The previous picture was created to be easily visible. Squint your eyes, adjust your focus, move closer or farther back, if you really need to. But, more than likely most people can see the words with ease in the preceding image. If you have the right perspective, the message pops right out!

It's appropriate Hunter said only *once in a while* you may get shown the light. There are no <u>absolute</u> guarantees here! Just like in the prior picture, there may be times one can't see the light. Many of us search for meaning—an answer to a prayer, or even a subtle "sign" making sense of our chaotic world. Often there is no answer to fathom. Why did I lose my soul mate? Why did that innocent child die? Why am I suffering from a disease? These are the types of questions most of us have (or will have) asked at some time in our lives. Occasionally there just doesn't appear to be answer. Even theologians wrestle with an explanation of this kind of difficult stuff. The problem of evil and suffering, with its horrific experiences, can contradict the idea of an omnipotent God, a great Spirit, a benevolent universe, or even a jolly Santa Claus—ho ho! Sometimes we just don't know the answer to many of life's hardest questions. But we still spend a great deal of our life trying to make sense of it all.

Once, I received some noteworthy relationship advice written on a bathroom stall; the best Chinese food I ever ate was served in a bamboo shack while I was waylaid in the middle of the Amazon jungle; and an amateur psychic medium diagnosed me with a medical issue my primary care physician only confirmed many years later. Those examples have reinforced the idea that wisdom, revelation, insight, and even great Kung Pao Chicken, don't always come from expected sources. Occasionally, I have seen the light. Sometimes, I haven't. Just as another more famous verse by the same song writer says, *"sometimes the light's all shining on me / other times I can barely see"* ("Truckin'"). Sometimes not always, I do get wisdom in the most unusual places, if I have the right attitude. This has been one of the great lessons of my life.

*"The wind in the willows played tea for two /
The sky was yellow and the sun was blue /
Strangers stopping strangers just to shake their
hand /
Everybody's playing in the Heart of Gold Band /
Heart of Gold Band"*

from "Scarlet Begonias"

Chapter 6

*"Everybody's braggin' and drinkin' that wine /
I can tell the Queen of Diamonds by the way she shines /
Come to daddy on an inside straight /
Well I got no chance of losing this time /
No, I got no chance of losing this time"*

From "Loser" 1971
by Robert Hunter and Jerry Garcia

The song "Loser" is one of the very best stories told in a
Hunter lyric. It is a great example of the Grateful Dead's tales
of the "*old, weird America*," a term coined by Greil Marcus to
describe the strange rural, blues and folk music featured in
Harry Smith's *Anthology of American Folk Music* (1927-1932).
Marcus calls the "*old, weird America*" the odd yet familiar
underbelly of American history. In that gritty America, we meet
hucksters, gunslingers, gamblers, hobos, fallen preachers,
outlaws, drunks, and an assortment of other scoundrels. Upright
and well-behaved citizens rarely made the headlines then or
now.

In the narrative of the song "Loser," we plop down at a poker game table, listening to the thoughts and words of a vain cardshark. Many other songs in the band's repertoire refer to cards, dice, or laying odds. Actually, there is a lot of gambling! In fact, no less than fifteen times did the Dead do a ditty about dice, doubling down, or other, gambling terms and stories.[1] Here are just a few references to games of chance in other popular Grateful Dead songs: "*I been gambling here abouts / for ten good solid years*" ("Deal"), "*Come on boys and gamble / Roll those laughing bones*" ("Candyman"), "*You know my uncle, he starts a friendly game / High-low jack and the winner take the hand*" ("Me and My Uncle"), "Sittin' plush with a royal flush, aces back to back," ("Ramble on Rose"), "'*You've got to play your hand' / Sometimes your cards ain't worth a dime / If you don't lay 'em down*" ("Truckin'"), "*we sat down for a game / I cut my deck to the Queen of Spades / but the cards were all the same*" ("Dire Wolf").

Despite America's puritanical past, gambling has always been part of our history. It is also a great metaphor for life's ups and downs, risks and rewards, and wins and losses. Like gambling, much of life is about luck and the fickle finger of fate.

In this song, we encounter the loser of the title, who is the song's narrator and protagonist. A trademark of Hunter's lyrics was we come to see the world from another's point of view. At times we are led to empathize with an under class of unsavory characters.[2] The loser in this song has few redeeming qualities. He is a pathological con man. He traded love for money, "*Put your gold money where your love is, baby.*" As simply a source of funds, his lover doesn't know he will abandon her and "*get up in the morning and go.*" Brazen con artistry! Even as he dismisses the blowhards in the game as "*braggin' and drinkin' that wine,*" he himself indulges in the same hypocritical behavior. "*I can tell the Queen of Diamonds by the way she shines,*" is an impossible task. His claims this is the "*last fair deal in the country*" and "*you'll never find another honest man,*" are all lies. But the crux of the song is his repeated grandiose claim "*Well I got no chance of losing this time. No, I got no chance of losing this time.*"

The loser pleads to the cards "*Come to daddy, on an inside straight.*" His big gamble is for a rare winning poker hand.

In five card poker, an inside straight is a draw where a missing card would fit in the <u>middle</u> of five consecutive cards regardless of suit. Since he is hoping for a queen, his hand is either ace, king, jack, and ten or king, jack, ten, and nine. Only a queen would complete both of these sequences of cards. (If all his cards were all diamonds, it would be a "flush" or even a "royal flush.") The successful draw would be one queen from

the remaining forty-seven cards. This is a low probability hand. The odds are 4 queens / 47 remaining cards = 9 percent. This would be a risky bet. Although the gambler claimed that he had *"no chance of losing this time,"* the actual probability <u>against</u>

drawing the needed card and thus losing was ninety-one

percent. The song never resolves the outcome of this particular

card game. But, the title "Loser," implies the conspicuous result.

Our cardshark in this song is guilty of the sin of hubris.

In its modern usage, the word "hubris" denotes excessive pride

or overconfidence. Hubris drives people to overstep limits,

in a way which leads to their downfall. The concept is familiar

throughout world literature. The Greek legend of Icarus involves

an iconic case of hubris. Icarus is given artificial wings made

of wax and feathers so he can fly. Due to his pride, Icarus

ignores warnings and flies too close to the sun, melting his

wings, falling from the sky, and drowning in the sea. Aesop's

Fables (600 B.C.) also cautioned of hubris through stories like

the "Tortoise and the Hare." The race between the tortoise and

hare resulted in a triumphant turtle, embracing not hubris, but

the opposite characteristics: humility, patience, and persistence.

These virtues have been passed in the story of the Tortoise

and Hare to modern times through a number of sources from

the *McGuffey Reader* to Disney cartoons. Even the ancient

Bible warns, "*pride goes before destruction, a haughty spirit

before a fall*" (Proverbs 16:18). Robert Hunter followed this well

established literary tradition in this cautionary song. *"Well I got no chance of losing this time*," is our gambler's brash hubris speaking.

Morality is the belief that some behavior is right and other behavior is wrong. Certainly the Grateful Dead winced at directly preaching to others about how to live in regard to right and wrong (unlike many bands from the '60s). But, a lot of songs from their folk tradition often took a perspective on the human struggles with morality.

> **Hunter recognized every child who begs for a bedtime story knows a great story (or song) will tell something fundamental about life. It is told not in a pat, preachy way, but in a much deeper way embodied in the behavior and skin of colorful characters.**

Our gambler was one of those characters with a living moral message. The song "Loser" is a backhanded morality tale about the virtue of humility. Perhaps if the gambler in the song had more of it, the song would not be called "Loser" and the outcome not so negatively implied. The song has served as a forewarning to me and others against falling victim to the same character flaw.

It is difficult to write about how this lyric has informed me. As a preventative, I would have to write about things I did not do and behavior deterred. Kind of challenging. But, most of us can give plenty of examples where we've proceeded way ahead of our own skis and regretted it later. Mark Twain wrote, "*When I was a boy of 14, my father was so ignorant I could hardly stand to have the old man around. But when I got to be 21, I was astonished at how much the old man had learned in seven years.*" Big servings of humble pie make most of us able to relate to Twain's more mature insight. As an adult, I am responsible for a string of prideful behaviors which left broken relationships, job loss, and other general screw ups. Most of us who have spun on this planet for any great length of time can confess to similar fiascoes.

Another prevailing lesson can be learned from the song. It is a harsh wake up for a child to realize life is not all teddy bears and comfy blankets. One sign of maturity is the unpleasant realization that there are some really bad actors among us.

The song "Loser" reminds me not all people have my best interests at heart. The loser was not only full of hubris, but also a classic con artist, even if he conned himself.

The actions of these crooks are anything but glamorous. Each year, researchers estimate millions of Americans are victims of fraud. Consumers reported losing more than $5.8 billion to fraud in 2021, a seventy percent increase over the prior year according to the Federal Trade Commission.[3] The cost of fraud is not purely financial as illustrated in the aftermath of Bernie Madoff's ponzi scheme. It wasn't just a few rich people whose bank accounts were drained. Madoff reduced tens of thousands of retirees to ruin, forced charities to close, made hospitals cut back on the care, wrecked the lives of many people who'd never even heard of him, and even caused some to commit suicide.[4]

The psychologist Maria Konnikova, is the author of *The Confidence Game* (2016).[5] She contends scam artistry is one of the oldest tricks in human history. It exploits a basic human trait—the predisposition to trust others. Thus, human nature is on the side of these masters of deception when it comes to defrauding their marks and contributes to the con's enduring success. Unfortunately, many people are too eager to put their trust in a swindler.

Konnikova claims there are three core traits con artists share, predictably, all of which can be seen in Hunter's lyrics. These personality traits, referred to as the "Dark Triad," are necessary ingredients for the worst kinds of malevolent actors. The three traits are psychopathy (lack of empathy), Machiavellianism (a manipulative mindset), and narcissism (excessive self-love). Some mixture of these traits appear in every con artist, including our loser in the song.

Out of the Dark Triad, psychopathy is the inability to process emotion like other people. To a true psychopath, our suffering means nothing. There is no empathy, remorse, or conscience. When psychopaths experience something, which would horrify most people—their pulse stays steady, their sweat glands normal, their heart rates low. Our loser possesses the traits of a psychopath. In particular, he orchestrates a classic "Blow Off," the final stage in the timeline of a typical scam. That is the point when the hustler disappears after a dreadful deed is done. Likewise, our gambler reports, "*I know a little something you won't ever know / ....Gonna get up in the morning and go.*" The loser planned to jilt his lover and make a secret getaway. There is lack of empathy and no remorse shown to the lover he plans to swindle and abandon.

Machiavellianism occurs when someone uses the tools of persuasion and deception to finagle what he wants at someone else's expense. To the Machiavellian, the ends justify the means. Being able to persuade others to do what you want them to do without their awareness of it, is a key to the con's success. Certainly, this trait appears in the song. Our loser attempts to deceive his lover with these words:

> *"All that I am asking for is ten gold dollars /*
> *And I could pay you back with one good hand /*
> *You can look around about the wide world over /*
> *And you'll never find another honest man"*

To the lover, ten gold dollars was to appear as a good investment in a trustworthy man's expertise at poker. Obviously, it was all a lie and the lover is being conned. Finally, the swindler cajoles her with the plea, *"Put your gold money where your love is, baby / Before you let my deal go down."* Those words are a final emotional squeeze on the heart of the unsuspecting sucker.

The last trait of the Dark Triad is narcissism. One has to have an overinflated sense of self in order to rationalize conning others. A common sign of people with narcissism is the belief that they are superior to others and deserve special treatment, i.e. <u>entitlement</u>. Despite the harm inflicted on others, the con artist believes he <u>deserves</u> the rewards of a successful swindle. Again, this trait is evident at the card table in our song. The loser claims to be superior to the other poker players. He knows things they don't know and claims special insight to be able to spot a *"queen of diamonds by the way she shines."* Most telling, however, is the narcissistic claim *"Well, I got no chance of losing this time."* Undoubtedly, the loser believed his own b.s.—he was surely entitled to be the winner.

No one knows precisely how many active con artists there are in the world. But, P.T. Barnum famously claimed, *"There's a sucker born every minute."* There are many people who thrive in taking advantage of these suckers' naivete, a harsh reality some refuse to face. But, all of us encounter con artists in our lives. The stakes today for us are usually much higher than the *"ten gold dollars"* of the loser's game.

My loss of innocence occurred in high school when I paid a guy $100 for the promise of a great new stereo system. The con took my money and moved to California. I never again saw him, my new stereo, or my money. I chalked it up as an early and important lesson about life. Even savvy and sophisticated folks can be conned. Sadly, I watched my own father (who should have known better) give $10,000 to a con artist who promised to double his money. Of course, it was too good to be true.

The internet and social media have become a bonanza for the dishonest. How many of us have received an email from a Nigerian prince to open our bank account for his riches? This is an example of the technique of "phishing." The swindler attempts to acquire sensitive data, such as bank account numbers, through a fraudulent solicitation. Amazingly, some people still fall for this phishing con as their bank accounts are drained by the so-called Nigerian prince.

Today, the most popular phishing template out there is the fake invoice technique. This scam relies on fear and urgency, pressuring an end user to submit a payment for goods or services they've never even ordered or received. I assume the odds are really much like fishing, i.e. throw out enough bait and some outlying creature will eventually bite. Send such a fake invoice to enough people, a few will pay it without question. I receive these fake invoices regularly in my email. As far as I know, I've not fallen for it yet.

Other forms of con artistry now use our ubiquitous phones. Many of us have received spoofed calls from the IRS, banks, and police departments. Here impostors use threats from seemingly legitimate agencies to manipulate their victims. This problem has gotten so bad official mail from the Social Security Administration today states the following:

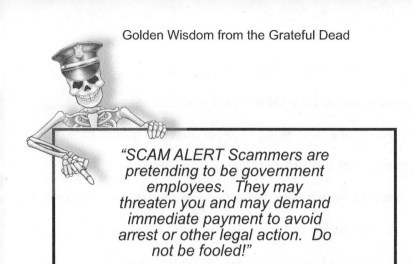

"SCAM ALERT Scammers are pretending to be government employees. They may threaten you and may demand immediate payment to avoid arrest or other legal action. Do not be fooled!"

I fear for those less skeptical than myself. What if my tech-challenged elders received such a call?

Other types of unwanted spam—telemarketing, and robocalls—are now a real nuisance. Some estimate spam accounts for about twelve calls per month per person.[6] Yet others report getting one of these spam calls every five minutes. Because of the volume of spam, most of us are forced to use some special software on our phones to screen out these illegitimate calls. In the past three months my spam filter has blocked over three hundred such calls on my phone, despite my number being on a National Do Not Call Registry. These are frequent and real encounters with con artists.

Whether via card games, business deals, internet grifts, or phone scams, no one can entirely escape the fact there are dishonest people in the world who want to take advantage of us. This realization contributes to a sobering loss of innocence, especially for anyone from the idealistic flower power generation. The song "Loser" tells the quaint story of one man's con at the poker table. Apparently, the rules of chance and his own hubris thwarted the cardshark's successful swindle, as the name of the song implies. Other cons could be more successful, at our expense. Hopefully lessons learned from Hunter's lyrics will help prevent that shake down. The song "Loser" makes me view the world with a more open-eyed realism. When someone tells me they, *"got no chance of losing this time"*—I am probably dealing with another loser.

Chapter 7

"Wave that flag, wave it wide and high"

From "U.S. Blues" 1974
by Robert Hunter and Jerry Garcia

The term "patriotic music" for Americans is usually exemplified by the march "Stars and Stripes Forever" by John Phillip Sousa, the "National Anthem," Irving Berlin's "God Bless America," or in more recent decades, Lee Greenwood's "God Bless the USA." This music accompanied with balloons, banners, and liberty bells proclaims the valor, purity, and justice of the American ideals. Despite some over-enthusiastic jingoism, these songs stir the emotions of most red-blooded Americans. Yet for Dead Heads, nothing gets the heart pumping more than hearing the band's "U.S. Blues" on the Fourth of July. It is the Grateful Dead's own twisted tribute to our red, white, and blue homeland. It was no accident the Dead's most famous logo, the Steal your Face skull and lightning bolt, shared the same three colors with Old Glory and the same number of stripes on the flag as points on their bolt of electricity. The Grateful Dead encouraged us to wave that psychedelic flag wide and high. The message to me is America, with all its peculiarities and flaws, is a uniquely great country. I believe the Grateful Dead was well aware of their nurturing homeland. Garcia said, *"...we're here to say that you can get away with it, and that in fact this is the place."*[1] Only the idealistic freedom loving USA could provide the fertile soil upon which the iconoclastic band could emerge and flourish for fifty years.

Many recognize the roots of the Grateful Dead easily stretch backwards from Ken Kesey to Jack Kerouac. Both of these writers were infected by a 20th century American Romanticism. That philosophy was preoccupied with notions of individualism, freedom, egalitarianism, optimism, and the exploration of new frontiers. Kerouac's writing spawned a generation of beatniks who abandoned Eisenhower's backyard barbecue. Many hit the road in search of a wilder and more authentic America. Kesey's magic bus trip mirrored Kerouac's *On the Road* westward adventures. Kesey and his tribe of Merry Pranksters searched for their country in the opposite direction, going West to East.

Although geographical expansion had ceased, thanks to pioneers like Kesey, thousands of intrepid Americans were encouraged to cross the boundaries of consciousness imposed by the mainstream society. Psychedelic pathfinders traversed new frontiers of "inner space." Kesey stated regarding his own acid exploits, *"this was as American as you could get because we were exploring a new territory—just the same way we went to the moon or sent the Lewis and Clark expedition.."*[2] The bubbling steaming electric Kool-Aid, originally fueling the Grateful Dead, came out of this American milieu. Sam Cutler, a manager for the band, recognized the unique national linage of these artists:

> *"The Grateful Dead, I think my view of it was, they were attempting to redefine, as every generation of American artists does, what it means to be an American artist, what in fact it means to be an American. Artists in America constantly struggle with this...they want to define what America is.*

They want to discover what America is. They want to find some clue to what it means to be American."[3]

In this tradition of rediscovering or redefining America, "U.S. Blues" was the Dead's own irreverent national anthem. In 1974, the song was released on their *Mars Hotel* album and was played live 325 times. Despite its name, the song was not really a blues tune. "U.S. Blues" is more of a swinging shuffle particularly appropriate for dancing and shaking bones.

The context of the song is interesting. In the mid-seventies, the U.S. had recently withdrawn from Vietnam, the Watergate scandal was unseating Nixon, the economy was stagnant, and the country was entering a national malaise. The flower power era of the Summer of Love and the Woodstock Generation were long over—"*summertime done, come and gone*"—and young people had become increasingly disillusioned and pessimistic. Understandably, patriotism was at a low ebb. But, the Grateful Dead was basically considered "apolitical" and never aligned themselves with any of the partisan hot air of their day.[4]

Perhaps the Dead's early politics were off the chart as opposed to being apolitical. In the *Last Whole Earth Catalog*, Steward Brand (a former Merry Prankster) articulated a strategy of the day, which was probably congruent with the band, "*You don't change a game by winning it or losing it or refereeing it or observing it,"* he claimed. *"You change it by leaving and going somewhere else and starting a new game from scratch"* (Brand, 1971, p. 35). In keeping with this do-it-yourself ethos, rather than change the external political world, the band wanted to create one to their liking.

From early on, the Grateful Dead was more interested in promoting a homespun utopia composed of a loose extended family. Ideally, their new world would be based upon the all-American values of life, liberty, and the pursuit of happiness coupled with lots of fun. It would be informed, at least in part, by being "high" in all of its meanings. Although lacking any dogma, there was something conspicuously spiritual about their vision.[6] They were not concerned with negative and contentious politics, but were searching for something much more positive—an alternative and better way of life. This country fortunately provided the necessary and unique landscape for their practice. Garcia stated, *"We're basically Americans, and we like America, we like the thing about being able to express outrageous amounts of freedom."*[7] Just a few years before, anti-war protesters were burning the American flag. But now the Grateful Dead was encouraging their fans to wave the red, white, and blue proudly.

Throughout its entire career, the Grateful Dead maintained an ambiguous but appreciative relationship with America. Jerry Garcia acknowledged his heritage as well as the dark side of the country's history, *"What we do is as American as lynch mobs."*[8] Other major West Coast bands of the '60s were less nuanced. For example, the Jefferson Airplane, a fellow Bay Area band, eventually had utter contempt for their own version of a dystopic Amerika (*"Up Against the wall motherfucker"* from the song "We Can be Together," 1971). But by the early 1970s, the Jefferson Airplane, along with other more political bands, came off as excessively strident and creatively bankrupt. But, the Grateful Dead's appreciation of their own American heritage gave the band an ample artistic foundation for creating an intelligent and interesting body of work, which would last the long haul.

> **By rejecting the overly simplistic stance of other '60s bands, they accidentally discovered a rich vein into the heart of Americana based on the country's own cultural myths and musical forms. As a result, the Grateful Dead's appeal to young Americans was almost as instinctive as grandma's apple pie.**

In the song "U.S. Blues," Robert Hunter brilliantly co-opted one of most powerful public-relations images of the federal government—Uncle Sam. Uncle Sam was the fictional upright citizen who was recognized by all Americans—the physical embodiment of all those John Philip Sousa marches. He was inflexible and austere and would never submit to totalitarian forces. If provoked, he would rear up with great anger and smite the enemies of democracy. *"He's sort of like the godfather figure of American culture. So we actually have a fair bit of respect for him,"* according to Bob Weir.[9] By poking the feds in the eye, Hunter provided a new fearless leader in the re-invented psychedelic personification. This one is alive not because of sacrifice or noble valor but because he *"learned to duck."*

Hunter's Uncle Sam is both confident and comedic. His pulse wouldn't budge under any circumstances. Garcia sang, *"I'm Uncle Sam, that's who I am / Been hidin' out in a rock and roll band."* So imagine this—Jerry Garcia (a.k.a Captain Trips wearing a star spangled top hat)—the pot smoking, acid-eating, hippie, rock star, and spiritual adviser of the '60s counterculture revolution—cast mockingly in the role of Uncle Sam, the symbol of the establishment, the USA, and all its military might.[10] Uncle Sam was appropriated from the drab and conservative establishment to a much more colorful icon – one who ditched the narc-style shiny black footwear for more patriotic Elvis-like, "*red and white / blue suede shoes.*" Watch it! Both P.T. Barnum and Charlie Chan were famous victims of this dude's

I'll drink your health, share your wealth, run your life, steal your wife.

shakedown. With murky motives, he'll now focus on you and "*Shine your shoes / light your fuse.*" Be careful—this Uncle Sam is morally dubious. If you give him five, he may take a ten-spot from your back pocket. The old patriot is a trickster, con man, and reprobate who'll "*drink your health / share your wealth / run your life / steal your wife.*"

Ultimately in the song, he steps off of his high horse, identifies with every American and with an open kimono admits,

"We're all confused / what's to lose?" This was the new Uncle Sam – colorful and free, animated and inviting, with a sense of humor. He doesn't have all the answers and is only making it up as he goes along – just like everyone else in America. This was the classic Grateful Dead stance of shrugging off authoritarian leadership and not preaching to others about how to think or live. *"Wave that flag wave it wide and high,"* indeed. Who wouldn't want to join the fun with this crazy song and dance man?

During their flag waving celebration, the Grateful Dead resisted alignment with any major political party or social movement. The politics of the '60s was pathetic according to Garcia (Goodman, 1989, p. 54). Consequently there was a decision to deflect divisive partisan politics. Instead, the band was much more interested in <u>inclusion</u> and bringing people together in a joyous jubilee, rather than dividing folks with quarrelsome politics. Jerry Garcia even told the chief wordsmith, Robert Hunter, to avoid political themes in their music.[11] Supposedly to the band, their politics like their religion, were mutually considered private and personal to each individual band member. Their stage was treated as near sacred space not to be defiled as a podium for any lectures or sermonizing from anyone, including the band members themselves. Phil Lesh explained their reticence to proselytize:

> *"Because we felt that what we were doing was more — I hate to use that word because it's almost a cliche — religious. What we were doing was religious in the sense of the word, which means to bind together. We were trying to create a community of spirit with the music and the political harangue and — again, it was just like a cop trying to tell people what to do, legislate morality or legislate private behavior. It was just anathema to us."* [12]

However, Jerry Garcia did not hesitate off stage to express his own political opinions. Garcia stated in an interview with Dennis McNally, that LSD had an early profound impact on him far superseding politics. As a result, he was unable to buy into any "us vs. them" mentality. He was compelled to address all people as unique individuals, instead of voting blocks or political parties.[13] In an interview with *Rolling Stone* in 1989, he spoke of his disdain for American politics and flat-out admitted he didn't even bother to vote. He is famous for saying regarding our two-party system (a choice between Michael Dukakis (D) and H.W. Bush (R) at the time), *"I don't feel there's anything to vote for yet. Constantly choosing the lesser of two evils is still choosing evil"* (Goodman, 1989, p. 54).

Interestingly, thirteen years after the passing of Garcia, three band members (Bob Weir, Phil Lesh, and Mickey Hart) did reunite for a one-time-only event in order to lend support to the

Democratic candidate, Senator Obama, on February 4th, 2008. The song, "U.S. Blues" was the encore for the evening. This was a highly exceptional event in the band members' history, I believe. No telling what Garcia would have thought of their partisan endorsement. I do know he was anti-authoritarian and reluctant to dictate his rules to any others, including his own bandmates.

Regarding political parties, given the '60s atmosphere of free love, experimental drug use, and anti-war activism you'd think the modern-day Democratic Party would be the natural home for their fans. But fifty years after the band's inception, the *Washington Post* explained you'd be wrong about the Dead Heads' political demographics today. A poll conducted in June 2015 found the band was popular across party lines. This is especially surprising in our hate-filled partisan era. Yet, no sharp partisan animosity has existed among Dead Heads, at least in my experience. Surprisingly at that time, Republicans were actually just as likely to be Grateful Dead fans as Democrats, with thirty-two percent and thirty-one percent respectively having favorable opinions of the band.[14]

Perhaps, the unexpected appeal of the Dead to the GOP may be explained by their libertarian-leanings. Regarding that liberty, when Garcia was asked how Dead Heads should behave at the band's concerts, he grudgingly replied, *"Do what you want, man. Just don't stand on anybody's head."*[15] That was Jerry's jive version of the Golden Rule, *"Do unto others as you would have them do unto you"* (Matt: 7:12). Obviously, that spiritual maxim transcends partisan politics and may appeal to Republicans and Democrats alike – along with Rastafarians, Pedestrians, Fruitarians, Unitarians, Equestrians, Libertarians, and any other one-off political or social group.

It is interesting that among their more famous fans, some well-known politicians from <u>both</u> sides of the aisle, have publicly embraced the band. Their political differences are extreme. Yet they are united in intense love for this music. That is a wonderful phenomena attesting to the reconciling power of music, specifically to the soundtrack of the Grateful Dead. Perhaps, the ongoing music and ethos of this rock band may be part of a healing balm for the deep political wounds in our country today. Truly, *"We're all confused / what's to lose?"*

Part of the band's success has been attributed to their inclusiveness. As a result Dead Heads have always been a more diverse bunch than their latter day stereotypes would suggest. Despite their common portrayal as burnt-out, stoned, free-loaders – which of course there are some – most fans functioned well in mainstream society and simply wore their tie-dye and let their hair down in the sanctuary of a Dead show. There they could wave their freak flag and *"wave it wide and high,"* among friends. Although mostly white and middle-class, Dead Heads have always come from all walks of life, economic status, and day jobs. I've known attorneys to zookeepers—"a" to "z"—who were devoted Dead Heads. Bob Weir was asked in 2019 *"What is a Dead Head?"* In his own awkward fashion, he responded:

> *"There are all kinds of Deadheads. You got tech guys, you got CEOs, you got gas station attendants, you got – you know – probably serial murderers. Not a lot of 'em. All kinds of folks... They're a certain kind of person who requires a little adventure in their lives and therefore they require a little adventure in the music they listen to, and we're happy to provide that for them."*[16]

Probably, they should have discriminated more regarding those serial murderers. But oblivious to those differing backgrounds, most Dead Heads considered themselves to be bozos on the same bus, at least at Dead shows. There was a cartoon closeness permeating the concert crowd and giving all a sense of being part of one large extended family wherever the band played. At those concerts strangers really did stop strangers *"just to shake their hand"* and <u>everyone</u> was welcomed into the *"heart of gold band"* ("Scarlet Begonias").

As a result of the Grateful Dead's wide welcome to a truly BIG TENT, today there is little unanimity on any subject among Dead Heads. The exception is a shared commitment to the music, the band, and their values. Check out any internet discussion group for Dead Heads. Opinions, nit picked minutia, pro and con diatribes, some erudite insight, and infrequent flashes of wisdom, all abound among this devoted tribe. A broad spectrum of thought has always followed the band from their own boardroom to online forums today. To any Dead Head, sincere appreciation of the music rises above social status, job title, religion, or politics. This unifying resolve has been recognized as a major key to the band's success. *"By being open and inclusive themselves, the Dead inspired the same spirit in their community of fans – and this allowed the number of Deadheads to grow and grow"* (Barnes 2011, pp 92-93).

The Grateful Dead helped me to be proud of my heritage. Yet, I recognize that the United States is far from perfect. Our history is pretty ugly and we have a host of current problems, which need fixing. But, I don't believe more intense partisanship and the resulting division are the solution. It doesn't make sense that one political party is always right and the other side is always wrong or one side is good and the other bad. In my opinion, binary black vs white groupthink isn't really acceptable in any area of life other than modern American politics and cults. Bizarre! Note, there is something in the vast intersection between black and white where, "*Every silver lining's got a touch of grey*" ("Touch of Grey").

When diverse people are brought together without respect to race, creed, or any shibboleths, it thrills me today. Old family stories about the Great Depression when my grandparents provided food for their neighbors, still warm my heart. I became an instant fan in the '70s when the cosmic cowboy, Willie Nelson, brought the hippies and the rednecks together in Austin's dance halls. In 1973 the Grateful Dead expressed an all-embracing sentiment as they sang "*wake up to find out that you are the eyes of the world*" ("Eyes of the World"). Over a decade later, the song, "We are the World," was produced by Quincy Jones as a benefit for Africa. The passion and beauty of the song made it a worldwide anthem, which only could have happened in a less partisan time. Soon after in the same spirit of unity, I applauded Hands Across America. That event attempted to form an unbroken human chain across the country. Those were happier and more connected times.

The tragedy of 9/11 brought Americans and its elected representatives temporarily together as it had not been since World War II. Suddenly the next day, there was no road rage. People honked and smiled and flew the Stars and

Stripes from their car radio antennas. Today when horrible catastrophes like floods or hurricanes strike, the mostly-volunteer relief efforts are offered indiscriminately. In recent crises, providers of humanitarian aid never ask the victim about their race, religion, sexuality, or politics. Those pigeonholes are trivial in life and death situations. These are just some of the unifying experiences which have given me a greater faith in our humanity and pride in our country. Hopefully, a future national tragedy will not be required to heal America's current divisions.

These lyrics from "U.S. Blues" and the spirit of the band that performed it, have reinforced my gratitude for my own country and those forces which bring people together, rather than divide us. When I recall the good ol' Grateful Dead uniting such a diverse group of colorful characters to celebrate and dance, it touches me at some deep spiritual level. Among those people, I am healed of disrespect and prejudice and provided the opportunity to express a greater degree of love for humanity. Perhaps this inclusion was part of the real spiritual contribution of the '60s which Jerry recognized and also appreciated.

I'm proud to be part of a group, which welcomed me as a member. In 1971 inside the band's second live album, *Skull &*

Roses, there was the first use of the term "Dead Heads" in the following message:

DEAD FREAKS UNITE

Who are you? Where are you?
How are you?
Send us your name and address
and we'll keep you informed
Dead Heads
P.O. Box 106
San Rafael, California
94901
Inside message on *Skull & Roses*
(1971)

I sent a letter back to San Rafael and responded to this public invitation to become a Dead Head way back at the time it was issued. Absolutely anyone could join. Even I, with all my own quirks and wacky ideas, have been included in this community of Dead Heads for over 50 years. I will continue to wave that flag and wave it wide and high indeed!

"*I'm Uncle Sam /
that's who I am
Been hidin' out /
in a rock-and-roll band*"

Chapter 8

"If you get confused listen to the music play"

From "Franklin's Tower" 1975
by Robert Hunter and Jerry Garcia

Robert Hunter wrote the lyrics to "Franklin's Tower" in

1975 with a view toward the upcoming American Bicentennial.

The celebration honored the creation of the United States as

an independent republic, culminating on July 4, 1976, with the

200th anniversary of the Declaration of Independence. The

song "Franklin's Tower" reflected national icons and the history

related to the American revolution.[1] It contains mixed imagery

of a bell that rings, a tower, four winds, fire, sand, hounds,

wildflowers, and child bell-ringers. The Grateful Dead used the

song as the final part of the second set trifecta medley of "Help

On the Way">"Slipknot">"Franklin's Tower." (See my chapter

"Paradise Waits on the Crest of a Wave" regarding "Help On the Way.") I doubt most Dead Heads today know any of the historic backdrop of the song. I am certain I adored the song long before understanding the symbolism within.

In Garcia's hands the infectious tune usually brought fans to their feet with a joyful sing-along chorus of "*Roll away....the dew, roll away....the dew, You've got to....roll away....the dew.*" However, one famous line in the song contains the reassuring words "*If you get confused listen to the music play.*" In concert, Garcia followed that line by weaving a guitar solo that provided the listeners an upward spiral of notes on which to focus their spellbound attention. This encouragement to "*listen to the music*" in times of confusion has been extremely useful on many occasions in my life.

Like many of Hunter's songs, the lyrics of "Franklin's Tower" are obscure enough and intended by the wordsmith to be interpreted many different ways. But this song is unique in the Dead's repertoire because it is the only song that Robert Hunter really ever explained to others. In 1996, Hunter wrote a response to a scholarly essay and refuted the idea that his lyrics were nonsensical. Hunter reluctantly expressed his original intent because, according to the author, it robs the listener of personal associations and replaces them with his own. He stated regarding his songs, "*I may know where they come from, but I don't know where they've been*" (Hunter, 1996). He certainly didn't know where those songs were going! To Hunter, exposing the original intent of his songs was like a magician revealing his tricks. The mystery would be gone.

Still, Hunter presented an exegesis of "Franklin's Tower" and cited some of his references in the song. He confirmed the historical figure, Ben Franklin, was the proprietor in the song. The cracked Liberty Bell that originally hung in the steeple of the State House in Philadelphia, Pennsylvania was the bell that "*may have one good ring, baby you can't tell*." Other references included the Constitution and Bill of Rights, Pete Seeger, the Bible, E.E. Cummings, Bonnie Dobson, an Easter hymn called "Roll Away the Stone," and the birth of his son. These all had their place in the song's original creation (Ibid.).

According to another author, even the phrase "*roll away the dew*" was probably tied to a real historical process.[3] Franklin supposedly created a technique called "dewing" that involved exposing a freshly cast bell to large quantities of steam while the bell was still hot. The steam preserved the integrity of the bell and assisted the cooling process, producing droplets of "dew" on the bell. After the dew was formed, the bell was rolled between large cotton sheets. Supposedly Franklin described this process as, *"rolling away the dew."*

In regard to the specific verse, *"if you get confused listen to the music play,"* Hunter stated his original intent. Should his

"It may have one good ring baby, you can't tell"

hyper-allusive train of thought in the lyrics become too confusing to process, he invited others to, *"listen to the music play."* That invitation acknowledged listening to both the performance of the tune itself and heeding the metaphoric ring of the Liberty Bell (Hunter, 1996). One ring of that bell symbolically reverberated in American history as one of the most resounding portrayals of our country's ideals. Given Hunter's permission above, I choose to interpret the phrase with undoubtedly the most common notion. "*Listen to the music play,*" to me is a general bid to find solace in music. With the constant barrage of disturbing news today, I have found myself calling upon this familiar Grateful Dead refrain and discovered it all the more relevant and inspiring.

Many have said that "*writing about music is like dancing about architecture.*" The two artistic expressions don't jibe very well. Nonetheless, in this entire book I offer my humble efforts to do so with the understanding that music is better experienced than described. However, music has always been important for me. I was born in the early '50s. As such I was fortunate to have lived when American music exploded for the burgeoning pig in the population python of us baby boomers. As a young kid, I listened and sang to my parents' records on my family's tinny HiFi (a piece of furniture as big as a washing machine today). Later a pocket-sized transistor radio allowed me to hear pop music under my covers, long after bed time.

The Beatles stormed American shores on the *Ed Sullivan Show* during my seventh grade. My mother said they'd never last because she couldn't understand their lyrics. But, young people like myself got it! I grew out my crew cut for a more mop-top hairstyle. The resulting hair wars created common household friction that often resulted in unwanted trips to the barbershop for young males like me. In the most extreme cases, I knew of intolerant parents who disowned their own boys for their long locks. How sad! Thus, this new music and their associated fashion trends fueled a generation gap between many parents and their kids in the '60s.

Mod rock groups in the British Invasion continued to create many new sounds marketed specifically for us boomers. Most of this music was heard on A.M. radio, between commercials, the Beatles, surf songs, Motown, folk singers, bubblegum pop, and lots of DJ chatter. Along with the Beatles and the Rolling Stones, the Yardbirds were one of the most copied English groups by thousands of American garage bands. Many young males (mostly) who identified with them and wanted to imitate their raw and aggressive sound picked up an instrument to channel new adolescent independence and rebellion. I certainly wanted to make music like those British chaps. So, I grew my hair longer, took drum lessons, learned to play a trap set (that my long suffering parents bought me), and formed a band. When my teen band played together well, I learned for the first time that making music can be an extremely exhilarating experience.

Young teens are in a formative age when we all confront the tyranny of sex and adulthood. This is true for most modern cultures and generations. We struggle to figure out our identity, and turn to the surrounding culture as sources of "cool"—the social currency for young teenagers. "*Fourteen is a sort of magic age for the development of musical tastes*," says Daniel J. Levitin, a professor of psychology at McGill University.

> "*Pubertal growth hormones make everything we're experiencing, including music, seem very important. We're just reaching a point in our cognitive development when we're developing our own tastes. And musical tastes become a badge of identity.*"[4]

It all may be just brain chemistry. But, it just so happened that I was at this susceptible age when music was really freakin' extraordinary. Some have called the year 1965: *The Most Revolutionary Year in Music* (Andrew Grant Jackson, 2015). Certainly, there was an explosion of artistic creativity during this time. My ears were wide open at this crossroads of budding adolescence and music history. You could hardly touch the A.M. radio dial at that time without soon hearing two and a half minutes of a seminal, groundbreaking classic recording.

As a response to the British Invasion, new American groups were becoming more popular. Most of this music originated from both coasts. From the East Coast came music from the likes of Bob Dylan, Simon & Garfunkel, Richie Havens, the Lovin' Spoonful, the Young Rascals, the Blues Project, the Velvet Underground, etc. From the West Coast, LA and Laural Canyon bands like the Beach Boys, the Byrds, Love, Buffalo Springfield, the Doors, and the Mamas and Papas created a southern California sound. Simultaneously, northern California exploded with the music of the Jefferson Airplane, Janis Joplin and Big Brother and the Holding Company, Country Joe and the Fish, Quicksilver Messenger Service, Moby Grape, and of course, the Grateful Dead.

This music expanded its audience to millions of young people in most large cities through the use of a new medium— F.M. radio. New F.M. radio stations switched from classical music, the original mainstay of the F.M. dial, to album-oriented rock music. When bands released new albums, their fans could listen to the whole thing on one of those stations. In my hometown of St. Louis, KSHE 95 became an early rock radio station of this kind. The first rock song played on KSHE when their format changed was the Jefferson Airplane's song "White Rabbit." In order to be close to this music, I got my first job at that radio station as a lowly office boy. I vacuumed the carpets, mopped the floors, and took out the trash to be a small part of this new wave. Later on in my college years, I became a DJ at a listener supported radio station in downtown St. Louis. I loved being surrounded by music and its ensuing culture.

I was a precocious teen and fortunate to experience early live performances of '60s music. I attended my first concert in 1966 when I was fourteen years old. The artist was Bob Dylan backed by the musicians that later became The Band. My next concert was watching the Beatles play at Busch Stadium in the summer of 1966. I have used that experience with the Fab Four as my own "cool" capital for the rest of my life. Later I attended concerts of most classic rock bands of the '60s. As I've written elsewhere (see Chapter 1, "*The Bus Came By and I Got On*") the first time I saw the Grateful Dead was 1968. It was kind of an underground acid test in the St. Louis Armory. Less than two hundred people attended. Although, I was pleasantly overwhelmed and bewildered at the time, it changed my life.

My musical interest continued to grow over time. Later I became a fan of many musical forms including folk, bluegrass, old-time music, Motown, funk, jazz, country, gospel, classical, world music, electronica, etc. My taste is quite eclectic. I learned to play three chords on the guitar when my kids were young and spent a lot of time singing and parlor picking with friends. I took banjo lessons when I was 40 years old. I played percussion in drum circles. In my 50s I played drums in a smooth jazz band, which performed in Austin restaurants. (The music was so "smooth," I considered it music to aid digestion.) With hopes of visualizing the sound and enhancing the performance, I later spent a decade doing semi-professional lightshows for Austin area bands. I've danced the two-step to country music and spent a few hours free-forming at raves. During the entire time, I remained a Grateful Dead fan. I could hear nearly all of the kinds of music mentioned above in just one Grateful Dead concert. The variety of their music helps keep them interesting today. The sound of the band, the lyrics, and the feelings I associate with it, have left a mark.

My appreciation of music is hardly unusual. But, enjoying music does seem to be unique to us humans. Unlike food or sex, music isn't necessary for our survival. But, it taps into the same parts of the brain as pleasure from these fundamental drives. Music can flood the brain with dopamine, a chemical associated with pleasure, motivation, and love. There is even some evidence that music lowers levels of the stress hormone cortisol and can be an effective tool to reduce anxiety.[6]

Remarkably, music penetrates the deep recesses of our brains according to Dr. Oliver Sacks. His essay "The Last Hippie" was the basis for a feature film, *The Music Never Stopped* (2011). It is a story about a patient with dramatic brain trauma that resulted in permanent amnesia. The condition left the young man in a catatonic and unresponsive state. Surprisingly, the patient exhibited a profound positive emotional reaction when exposed to live music at a Madison Square Garden concert. Coincidentally it was the music of the Grateful Dead, one of his favorite bands from his forgotten past. Even in the face of other devastating neurological problems like Alzheimer's disease, apparently some musical memory persists when all other memories are long gone.[7]

Music can be stripped to its barebone component of just a vibrational pulse—rhythm. Even in that primitive form, it maintains a power. This capacity of rhythm should not surprise since the movement of the planets, the circadian 24-hour cycle, the beat of one's heart all provide a cadence necessary for life. Mickey Hart, a Grammy award winning percussionist and half of the Dead's drum duo known as the Rhythm Devils, has written and spoken extensively on the subject of music as medicine and the function of rhythm in health.[8] In 2001, I attended a workshop put on by Hart and other famous percussionists including Arthur Hull, the father of the modern drum circle movement. During the workshop, I learned firsthand how rhythm can positively influence mood. All the drum beats and vibrational interplay kept me naturally high for weeks following that event.

Throughout history, music made a powerful impression on the human experience. In 1697, William Congreve wrote "*Music has Charms to soothe a savage Breast*" (often misquoted as "*Beast*"). Empirical and ethnological studies of music's effects show that it has a wide variety of reactions in different contexts. A constant theme suggests it has considerable transformative power for us humans.[9]

> **Of all the arts, music has the most immediate emotional impact on an audience, with an ability to change our normal consciousness.**

Yet, the effects of music can vary widely. For example, lullabies have long been used in every human culture to soothe and induce sleep for distressed babies. Other forms of music, like the Highland bagpipes, have been used as weapons of war. Pete Seeger made the song "We Shall Overcome" the unifying anthem of the Civil Rights movement in the 1960s. The theme of electronic rave music was to promote peace, love, understanding, and respect. But, other types of music have resulted in chaos and violence. In 1913, Igor Stravinsky debuted his ballet "The Rite of Spring." Though it is one of Stravinsky's most famous works, it also includes dissonant and aggressive sounds. His creation was met with harsh criticism, negative reviews, and...a riot. Today's heavy metal music often expresses anger and discontent and sometimes also results in mosh pit bloodshed. Gangster rap music, likewise, is born of anger and is focused on violent life in the ghetto.

Further, music can transform some people to go crazy. Nearly everyone has at least one song that sets their teeth on edge. Most of the time, those songs are easy to avoid. But, in 1989 repetitive loud music was forcefully blasted nonstop at Manuel Noreaga as torture to help oust him from his Panamanian dictatorship. The ultimate maddening earworm for many parents might be "It's a Small World" at the Disney parks. Maybe the reason that song crawls into the ear and nests so easily is because parents have often waited for hours in the hot sun for a short boat ride while the tune played in a constant loop. Perhaps the "Barney Song" is even more despised by younger parents. Some have even speculated that the "Barney Song" played backwards has evil lyrics.

Even the music of the Grateful Dead provides a smorgasbord of visceral experiences. I admit, I am not a fan of every one of their songs. I pick and choose from their enormous repertoire what I really like. In concert, I enjoy the variety of music played. From the soothing gospel-like sounds of "Broke Down Palace" to the harsh chords of "Viola Lee Blues," the music of Grateful Dead satisfied my entire emotional palete.

Music has been an antidote for the stress and confusion of the modern world. Playing music with others, whether in a drum circle, in a picking parlor, or in a garage band, can unequivocally be described as *the most fun I can have with my clothes on.* As a teen, it helped me eventually compose my off-beat identity. Music was played at my wedding. It was a refuge for me during my divorce. Mickey Hart created an album, *Music to Be Born By* (1989), as an aid for childbirth. When my mother was on her deathbed, I used other music to help with her transition in the opposite direction.

Most of us have been moved by a piece of music, experienced a life changing live musical performance, or found solace in playing an instrument or listening to a favorite artist. Music lovers have moments when a particular song or piece of music feels especially meaningful. I have a new favorite song each couple of months depending on my state of mind. How long has it been since music made your spine tingle? Music has given me a lot. Music has lulled me to sleep and also quickened my pace while exercising. It has transported my imagination to exotic and celestial places. It has shaken my sacrum with erotic passion. It has both brought tears to my eyes and great joy to my heart. During the COVID-19 pandemic, live music concerts broadcast over the internet and played in my living room were an oasis in an otherwise isolated and depressing time.

Remember "Franklin's Tower" was inspired by the historical imagery of 1776 and America's bicentennial. As such, it is a patriotic song. Today, there is simple optimism in Hunter's words, *"If you get confused listen to the music play."* If his song's symbolism was too bewildering, he offers us some sanctuary in sound. Although I've taken a broader approach about music here, Hunter's original thought included just one more ring of the American Liberty Bell. That bell can, *"turn night to day / It can ring like fire when you lose your way."* The resounding reverberation would proclaim freedom in the land. Because of that bell's ring, I've been privileged to live in a time and place to really enjoy great music in my leisure. I am well aware people in other generations and other countries have lacked the opportunities and resources, which I have savored. Frankly, I've often been struck by the irony that my father fought on Iwo Jima in WWII so that I could see the Beatles twenty years later. For that, I'm eternally grateful.

I've been amused that the rock music of my generation, often criticized by the extreme Right as being part of a decadent political plot to corrupt American youth, is now widely recognized to be an important factor that brought down the Iron Curtain.[10] Eastern European teenagers' desire for freedom, blue jeans, and western music crushed communist control in the late 20th century. Roll over Beethoven, indeed! Music can change the world. The sweet symbolic ring of the Liberty Bell, the true sounds of a gospel choir, a drum circle, a classical orchestra, the Fab Four, the Grateful Dead and more, have all provided powerful resonance in my own pursuit of happiness. As a great source of joy, I plan to continue to, "*listen to the music play,*" until my final crescendo.

Chapter 9

"Lately it occurs to me / What a long strange trip it's been"

From "Truckin'" 1971
by Robert Hunter, Jerry Garcia, Bob Weir, and Phil Lesh

The phrase, *"What a long strange trip it's been"*

(WALSTIB), is probably the most popular artifact from the

large cannon of Grateful Dead tunes. It is part of the chorus of

"Truckin'," released on the *American Beauty* album of 1970, with

words and music attributed to the committee of Robert Hunter,

Jerry Garcia, Bob Weir and Phil Lesh. (For brevity, I will again

refer to Hunter as the main author of these lyrics.) As one of

the most famous lines in rock and roll, it will be part of Hunter's

legacy long after we all have departed this world. It is deeply

etched in our culture. For decades it has been a popular quote

for countless high school year books, valedictorian speeches, and road trip eulogies. As baby boomers grow older, it has found new applications in retirement speeches. Recently, it's been an epitaph chiseled into some tombstones.

The phrase now appears to be a ubiquitous meme. Based on an Internet search, the *"long strange trip"* descriptive metaphor has been applied to an unending variety of peculiar things including personal computers, juvenile rheumatoid arthritis, Volkswagen Beetles, commercial banking, net neutrality, medical marijuana, the Chicago Cubs, the Tea Party movement, Covid-19, Walgreens, a supreme court justice, charter schools, and the Zika virus, just to mention a few examples. The phrase, *"What a long strange trip it's been,"* has been used in many films and TV shows including *That 70's Show* (1998, S04E20), *The Office* (2005, S03E07), *Dude, Where's My Car?* (2000), *Nashville* (2012, S05E02), and even *The Sopranos* (1999, S05E03). In the Grateful Dead circles, the phrase was used as the title of a 1977 greatest hits record. Also in 2017 it became the title of a critically acclaimed four-hour documentary movie on the band by Amir Bar-Lev and Martin Scorsese.

Supposedly, Robert Hunter was once chastised by a scholarly academic critic. Hunter was berated for using the apparent worn out cliché, *"long strange trip,"* in the chorus of his song "Truckin'." The songwriter explained to the confused professor that he'd actually <u>originally</u> coined the phrase and thus was innocent of that particular transgression.[1] In fact, fragments of Hunter's lyrics do invisibly permeate American life, like free-floating cultural oxygen. That is the ultimate measure of his wordsmithing success!

Widespread cultural approbation of this lyric indicates that it speaks for an awful lot of folks. Like others in our culture, WALSTIB has certainly embedded itself firmly in my consciousness. I believe my own embrace of this phrase has helped me better appreciate the meandering and unpredictable nature of my own trek. For most of us, life rarely proceeds in a highly predictable linear fashion. There are bumps, turns, and unexpected challenges with each step.

> **This is an important message I've tried to share with my own kids. I want them to understand it's really "ok" if things don't work out as planned and not to be hopelessly discouraged by dashed dreams. Instead, I want them to be resilient, open, and optimistic about the uncharted journey waiting for them to embrace.**

I will not try to recount here all of that long and strange history of the Grateful Dead. A number of great books already have well-documented interpretations of that story. But regarding the phrase WALSTIB, John Perry Barlow conceded the following:

> *"The real marvel is that the Grateful Dead made this declaration back in 1969. Considering all that went down in the four very weird decades since then, it seems obvious that we didn't know the meaning of long or strange at that point. (We did have a pretty firm grasp on the meaning of trip.)"*[2]

I think the <u>strangest</u> aspect of the Dead's long journey has been their transformation from an outlaw, counter-cultural, dope-smoking, acid-eating bar band into a hugely successful touring rock band. It's perplexing how they continually receive more and more popular mainstream acceptance. That is especially strange!

The first time I saw the Grateful Dead in concert was relatively early in their career and many years ago, nearly before dirt and sticks were invented. At that time, gasoline was $0.34 a gallon. A brand new Ford Mustang cost $2,707. Lyndon Baines Johnson, then the President of the U.S., had just announced the previous month that he would not be running for another term due to his persnickety problem in Southeast Asia. Three years before the moniker "Dead Head" was first used to describe their fans, my ticket to see the band cost me a whopping $3.00.

In flyover country between both coasts, few had heard of the Grateful Dead at that time. On the night I first heard them perform, the band played with full gusto for our small troop. As a popular bumper sticker later acknowledged, *"There is Nothing Like a Grateful Dead Concert."* While the notes from Captain Trip's guitar bounced off the walls of that concrete cavern like neon ping-pong balls—yes, we had a real good time. For many of us, it was our own Midwest acid test. For me, it was a life changing event. For the band, they were just barely getting started on their long strange trip.

A funny thing happened to this psychedelic sock-hop band in the next few decades. The Grateful Dead became really popular. Known for the same hippie ethos, live performances, and long improvisational jams, the band's fame grew organically. Older siblings and friends shared tribal tales and traditions, store-bought records, bootlegged tapes, and psycho-active substances to initiate newcomers into the grateful fold. During the remainder of the '60s and '70s, the Grateful Dead played intimate venues and theaters to a beloved and highly enthusiastic, but small audience.

By the mid-'80s, however, the Dead's popularity became viral. In 1984, Don Henley observed their expansive acclaim in a song, "*Out on the road today I saw a Deadhead sticker on a Cadillac*" ("Boys of Summer"). Dead Heads were showing up everywhere! From Patrick Leahy (liberal Democratic senator

Grateful Dead at the Warfield, 1980 ©Chris Stone gratefulphoto.com

from Vermont) to Tucker Carlson (conservative firebrand broadcaster), a wide variety of famous celebrities began to slowly and publicly embrace being Dead Heads themselves.[3] The growing impact of the band was even evident at many neighborhood grocery stores. In 1986, Ben and Jerry's ice cream named a new flavor, "Cherry Garcia," after the guitarist. The band's popularity swelled.

The next year, their secret was really shared with the release of the Grateful Dead's first and only Top 10 single with 1987's "Touch of Grey." (See Chapter 11 on "We will Survive"). It brought an influx of fans who forced the band to play in large arenas and sports stadiums. The new fans found the music to be an authentic foil to the slick big-haired prepackaged commercial rock and edgy new wave that dominated the day.

The newbies also discovered the scene around the band to be both inclusive, liberty loving, and a whole lot of fun. Dennis McNally observed these newcomers were welcomed to, *"the wildest party they have ever seen in their lives,"* at a Grateful Dead concert.[4] The sheer size of the band's traveling circus grew each year. By the early '90s, the Grateful Dead was one of the top-grossing bands of the day, bringing in millions of dollars in touring revenue alone, with additional money from merchandise and record sales. Knowing their history of wealth and fame never being the driving motives for the band, my head spins at their success.

Garcia was not entirely perplexed by their later popularity. He agreed with the quote from the movie *Chinatown* that, *"politicians, ugly buildings, and whores all get respectable if they last long enough."*[5] The musician applied the same overdue esteem to their new found prestige. Yet, according to Jerry, the band didn't sell out for their late commercial success. He insisted, *"The Dead hasn't changed much from our point of view, but the world has changed around it."*[6] That changed world included a growing fan base of more famous people. Academics, entertainers, politicians, and business people continued to come out of the closet as big admirers of the band. In 1992, Stonehenge Ltd., a New York neckwear manufacturer, introduced a tie collection based on Jerry Garcia's minimalist drawings and abstract paintings. That seemed especially odd since the guitarist's signature look was a black T-shirt and sweat pants. Apparently, Garcia seldom wore a tie in his entire life.

The fame of the band continued until the day Jerry Garcia died on August 9,1995. The most famous noninhaler and then President of the United States, Bill Clinton, in an *MTV* interview respectfully eulogized the Grateful Dead guitarist as a great talent and a genius.[7] From a counter culture outlaw to one who receives presidential postmortem acclaim—WALSTIB, indeed!

Yet even after the death of Jerry Garcia, the band became more popular and firmly embraced by mainstream America. Its long strange trip continued. Although the band semi-retired the name "Grateful Dead" in 1995, the music prevailed. Surviving band members formed the successive splinter groups The Other Ones, the Dead, and Furthur to keep both the music and their vibe alive. Each offshoot band drew huge crowds, indicating that there was still life in those old bones. I found a fundamental similarity existed among all the branches that sprung from the roots of the band: their music transported me to places other musical groups couldn't touch.

Twenty years later in 2015, the surviving band mates decided to get together one last time to honor their 50 year legacy, give the fans a few more shows, and officially retire the band name "Grateful Dead." On the final nights of those concerts, sold-out crowds packed in Levi Stadium and Soldier Field. Dead Heads bid Godspeed to a band that had a huge impact on music, popular culture, and most importantly—on their lives. The final celebration was a huge success, both musically and financially.[8] During that farewell concert, another President of the United States chimed in on the band. This time Barack Obama paid tribute to the long-running rock band with a message congratulating the group on their enduring legacy. Obama said the following:

> "Here's to fifty years of the Grateful Dead, an iconic American band that embodies the creativity, passion and ability to bring people together that makes American music so great. Enjoy this weekend's celebration of your fans and legacy. And as Jerry would say, 'Let there be songs to fill the air.'"[9]

Surprisingly, after a half century of performances capped by their goodbye concerts, the long strange trip still continued. Hundreds of Grateful Dead tribute bands sprang up and kept the music and spirit of the Grateful Dead alive.[10] All over the country, these bands played music mostly from the cannon of the Dead. They proved there was ongoing inherent power in the unique music itself. I doubt any other band could claim that degree of flattery.

A configuration of three surviving members (Hart, Kreutzmann, and Weir) into the band Dead & Company also persisted to carry the group's banner higher, tour the USA, and sell out venues with extraordinary live music. The music never stopped. From my perspective at Dead & Company concerts, the crowd, now multi-generational, resembled Dead Head crowds from past decades. Tie-dye T-shirts, kind veggie burritos, and even "nugs" and "doses" were all still traded in the parking lot. At a Dead & Company show, I felt enormous vindication as I heard an entire football stadium sing along with the words to Grateful Dead tunes. Five decades ago, I believed there was something extraordinary about the Grateful Dead. I was right! It was like having my favorite local sports team win the Superbowl.

Life Lessons in their Songs

In the summer of 2023, after eight years playing together (as long as the Beatles), Dead & Company announced their final tour. Over forty thousand people sold out Oracle Stadium in San Francisco to hear this band again bid goodbye. But, if the past is the best predictor of the future, the music will survive in new and unexpected forms for many years to come. The bus is still rolling after all this time!

One of the more heartwarming indications that this music is not likely to fade away soon concerns a new generation of young people who are singing these songs with fresh voices. In Austin for the past few years the Barton Hills Choir, made up of local 2nd through 6th graders, has been posting videos on youtube.com of their renditions of Grateful Dead music.[11] At this time, the Barton Hills Choir discography includes two CD volumes of Grateful Dead music sung by these children. I am now certain new generations of Dead Heads have emerged who were born long after the death of Jerry.

I am struck by the major paradox of this band's journey from an outlaw bar band to such a lucrative and culturally acceptable behemoth. From a meager audience of 125 fans to millions of Dead Heads, the band has been lauded by two Presidents and adored by grade school kids. I have witnessed this long and very strange trip. I don't believe it is near an end. Years from now, long after I am gone, the music and phenomena around this band will be respected by future generations.

What lesson can I draw from this long strange trip of the Grateful Dead? Unfortunately, our similar wealth and fame are not guaranteed. Everything won't necessarily end up "sweet and neat." It doesn't work that way. It seems the universe is not especially interested in maintaining our status quo or improving our lot in life. Instead, it will thrust change upon us.

In my lifetime, I've survived the impact of several earth shaking technical and cultural revolutions. Television, birth control pills, LSD, women's lib, personal computers, and the internet all had major impacts on my American milieu. Each created new challenges and opportunities. Some predict that artificial intelligence will be the next big thing.[12] No one knows for sure. But, big revolutionary changes like these are increasingly frequent. It took 100 years for landline telephones to become ubiquitous. It took eight years for smart phones to do the same. The speed of change has accelerated.[13] As a result, a life of unexpected twists and turns is now nearly as regular as clockwork.

This is especially true in the job market. Today, the U.S. Department of Labor reports that less than one half of college graduates find work in the field they studied in school. The average person will change jobs five to seven times during their career. One third of the workforce changes jobs every twelve months. In the very near future, artificial intelligence probably will threaten much greater disruption for the modern wage earner. Both now and certainly tomorrow, this change will be the rule, not the exception.

Most of us dreamed of a storybook white picket fenced future with two cars and a chicken in the pot, where we all could live happily ever after. Yet things didn't quite turn out as expected. Today, many of us didn't wake up in the gingerbread home we anticipated or with the people we assumed would join us. Fractured families, technological revolution, economic upheaval or health challenges have touched us all. These problems multiply when we include the experiences of our children and extended family members. No one is immune from the disruptive nature of modern life. Because of that, all of us find ourselves from time to time in circumstances we never expected.

Most often change comes with resistance. I've heard it said that the only ones who really like change are, *"babies with dirty diapers."* Yet, a major life transition can be a good thing. It closes one chapter of our lives and opens a new one. Change can promote growth and learning, make life interesting, and bring one closer to the fluid essence of life itself. But, these benefits are contingent on our reaction to change. We can view it as a benefit or a curse. When we spend too much time looking backwards, we miss out on the opportunities in front of us.

I love the mountains and I always thought I'd like to live in a high altitude pine forest in the beautiful Rockies. But, it hasn't happened—yet. I have missed the cool air, whispering trees, and beautiful vistas, as I've spent most of my adult life on the prairie in central Texas. To cope with my unmet expectations, some years ago I planted 600 six-inch pine trees on several acres I owned on this flat land. In this case, I took advantage of the opportunity I had, rather than focus on what I lacked. Since I didn't live among pine trees in the mountains as hoped, I brought the pine trees to me. Today, a small forest of pine trees over 100 feet tall and with trunks five feet in diameter stands in central Texas, because I tried to make the best of the unanticipated circumstances of my journey. Those trees, and the wisdom of the Grateful Dead, are part of the legacy I'd like to leave for my loved ones.

Too often, we think everyone else is moving in a smooth and successful path to their goals and only <u>my</u> life is muddled by misdirection and disappointment. In my opinion, this is a common illusion that leads to a lot of unnecessary self-loathing. J. R. Tolkien concurred that, *"Not all who wander are lost."* From my observations, rarely does anyone move in a straight line from point "A" to point "B." Instead, meandering twists and turns are more likely to get us to our destinations. This zig and zag is the real norm. As stated, the words WALSTIB have been inscribed in countless year books, speeches, eulogies, and even on tombstones. The reason that these words have been embraced by so many people, is because they speak of a near universal reflection of our human experience. Acceptance of this long strange nature of life's journey is an important component of mature wisdom.

"Truckin'--I'm going home /
Whoa--oh, baby, back where I belong /
Back home--sit down and patch my bones /
and get back Truckin' on"

from "Truckin'"

Chapter 10

"See here how everything / lead up to this day / and it's just like any other day / that's ever been"

From "Black Peter" 1971
by Robert Hunter and Jerry Gacia

I have never really thought of the Grateful Dead as being exceedingly ghoulish. However, their name undoubtedly scared many people. At a meeting to choose a band name in 1965, Jerry Garcia launched his finger at a random page in a *Funk and Wagnall's Dictionary* and landed on "GRATEFUL DEAD." What came next, as they say, is history. But, the term that Garcia chose actually referred to a specific genre of folklore. The ancient tale concerns a traveler who pays the debt of a corpse to provide for a decent burial. In turn, the ghost of the corpse repays the traveler with aid on his journey. Though a creepy legend indeed, it is essentially a lesson about good karma.

agreeable. **3** Expressing or denoting thankfulness; indicative of gratitude. [<L. gratus, pleasing] Synonyms: obliged, thankful. See AGREEABLE, DELIGHTFUL.LY adv. ---NESS noun.

GRATEFUL DEAD The motif of a cycle of folk tales which begin with the hero's coming upon a group of people ill-treating or refusing to bury the corpse of a man who had died without paying his debts. He gives his last penny, either to pay the man's debts or to give him decent burial. With a few hours he meets with a travelling companion w aides him in some impossible task, gets him a fortune, s s his life, etc. The story ends with the companion's on sing himself as the man whose corpse the other had b nded.

GRAT-I-FI-CA'-TION noun **1** The a gratifying; satisfying or pleasing. **2** Th ratified; specifically, in psychology xual

Yet the random band name allowed many to dismiss the Grateful Dead as a repulsive death metal group. Jerry Garcia said with a chuckle regarding their band name that, "*It turned out to be tremendously lucky. It's just repellent enough to filter curious onlookers and just quirky enough that parents don't like it*" (Jackson, 2000. p. 85). Certainly, the skeleton icons added to their spooky facade. But, to any knowledgeable listener, the band's aesthetic was far from pitch black. Nevertheless, it is hard to get a handle on the overall tone of their music. A Reddit discussion asked the question *"Do you think Grateful Dead songs are upbeat?"* As expected, the Reddit responses varied a lot. Users described the music with contradictory terms like *"happy,"* *"sad,"* *"creepy,"* and *"cheerful."*

The band produced a wide visceral spectrum of music. In their live performance, bright tunes like "Sugar Magnolia" and "Dancing in the Streets," were often juxtaposed with gloomy songs like "Death Don't Have No Mercy" and "Ruben and Cherise." For most Dead Heads the emotional impact of their music ranged from ecstatic joy to tears of cosmic woe. For every skull image that represented the band, there were also smiling cartoon dancing bear icons. For every "Dead" semblance there is also a "Grateful" aspect. Remember that many of their symbolic skeletons were entwined with living roses. One author wrote,

> *"The downbeat lyrics contrasted sharply with the band's festive concerts and broadened the band's repertoire and emotional range. They also connected the Dead to American roots music in a way that escaped many casual listeners and critics"* (Richardson, 2015, p.107).

But, there is no denying Grateful Dead music has a darker edge than most rock and roll. Death was a topic their music amply addressed. One source estimated that nearly three quarters of the songs Garcia sang featured lyrics about suffering and nearly half of those directly addressed death itself (Ibid, p.108). In "Cryptical Envelopment," Garcia seemed to sing of a psychedelic ritual that could be lifted straight out of Tim Leary's *Tibetan Book of the Dead*. In another ballad, the singer whimsically pleaded for a prehistoric beast not to murder him ("Dire Wolf"). A real life event at Altamont where "*in the heat of the day a man died of cold*" was lamented in the "New Speedway Boogie." In "Box of Rain," Hunter and Lesh pondered, "*Such a long long time to be gone / And a short time to be there.*" Even the taboo subject of suicide was recounted in the song "China Doll." There are many other examples of Grateful Dead tunes that didn't shy away from the important subject of our mortality. In the old-time folk music tradition that formed the background for both Hunter's and Garcia's song writing, death has always been great fodder for story telling. Thankfully, their music has been somewhat of an existential remedy for my own angst about the subject.

Although the old American songbook highlights murder ballads and fatal consequences, death is not a comfortable subject in our current culture. Most recognize that modern America is preoccupied with the preservation of youth and beauty. Our society clings to the illusion that youth and life can last forever. Generally speaking, the American attitude toward death is one of denial. A major factor contributing to this view is the fact that the end of life has now been hidden from us.

During earlier times, the dying remained at their homes and their primary caretakers were family members. Children were present along with everyone else throughout the dying process and the subsequent funeral preparations. The family often washed the body, built the coffin, and prepared the grave site. In the year 1900, the average American died at the age of 48.[3] In my grandparents' generation, infant mortality was so high new babies were often not named until after a first birthday. Following the death of most people in their own quarters, their bodies were regularly laid out for viewing in their home's front parlor. Modern medicine changed all that.

Today, most people die outside their home in a hospital room, too often unfortunately in the company of strangers. Increased mobility has separated siblings, parents, and grandparents and made it more difficult for the extended family to experience the dying process of loved ones. Also, much of modern medicine has treated death as a "failure," which should be mitigated with life-sustaining technology. Even grief has become unfashionable. In modern corporate settings, employees are typically given just three-days leave to make arrangements and grieve, even if it's a spouse or other close relative who died.[4] Then, employees are expected to go right back to resume normal work.

But, it is an earlier archaic era of the "old, weird America" that the Grateful Dead's rootsy album *Workingman's Dead* enshrined. This shadow world of gamblers, rogues, doomed lovers, con artists, and other unsavory characters was the folk fountainhead for many of the Hunter and Garcia tunes. It was there that "Black Peter" lived and died. During those earlier times, the sights, sounds, and smells of death were far more common and personal.

"Black Peter" is one of my favorite Grateful Dead songs. The song, like many of the Dead's, is an enigma subject to many equally valid interpretations. It's a partial first person narrative of a man (Black Peter) lying in bed with a high fever, ("*Fever roll up to a hundred and five*"). He's pretty sure that he is going to die, ("*I was laying in my bed and dying*"). But, he is surprised that he has survived another day, ("*One more day I find myself alive*"). The prognosis for the narrator in the song doesn't look good. He laments, "*tomorrow maybe go beneath the ground.*"

It is the haunting swell of a bridge in this tune that always grabs my attention. The music lifts in a wave, Garcia's voice strained, and the others harmonized:

*"See here how everything / lead up to this day /
and it's just like any other day / that's ever been /
Sun goin' up and then / the sun it goin' down /
Shine through my window / and my friends they come around /
come around, come around."*

It is a spine-tingling piece of words and music I have listened to, mulled over, and adored for over 50 years. This little snippet has provided for me a far-reaching understanding of the nature of my own life and demise.

> **Despite my own hubris and my important and undoubtedly preeminent role in the drama of my own life, my passage from this earth will be relatively insignificant. Like the passing of Black Peter, my exit will be like any other day.**

The band must have had an affinity for the song. It's ironic that "Black Peter" was performed at a rock and roll show at all. Maybe a parlor-picking guitar pull or some cowboys' campfire would have been more suitable. But, the Grateful Dead played this in concert nearly 350 times. It was the most played song from their *Workingman's Dead* era, even played

slightly more than the wildly popular song "Uncle John's Band."
"Black Peter" was among the top 30 in their entire rotation of
nearly five hundred songs.[5] Usually the song was played in the
band's second set,
though I doubt it was
ever the last song of the
night. I suppose, the
melancholy tone was no way to
end a Grateful Dead concert.
The song was too dark and
ambiguous. "Black Peter"
was usually played
between two upbeat
jams. What a hoot! While
most fans were given a few
moments of respite to catch their
breath, the song stood up and grabbed me by the neck and
shook me with existential angst.

 The bridge in the song speaks to me at various moments,
whether listening at a concert or to the stereo in my living room:
"*see here how everything lead up to this day...*" It's a sublime
moment, an epiphany, being lifted up to us on the culmination of
a life. Peter Wendel added regarding the personal impact of the

song that it never disappointed and was *"frequently melting me into a puddle of lysergic, self-reflective mush."*[6] It provides a reverence for the eternal force of death and its ability to render the memoir of a common man of no great lasting consequence. David Dodd, the author of the *The Complete Annotated Grateful Dead Lyrics*, commented on these words:

> *"There is so much packed into that simple set of lines, so much that a listener can unpack over a lifetime of listening, that you have to wonder how Hunter, at a relatively young age, could have come up with something so profound."*[7]

The songwriter was 28 years old when his song was first performed in 1969.

Part of the meaningful message of "Black Peter," conveyed largely via the bridge, is again in sympathy with some sacred text and traditions. The concepts of both impermanence and continuity are part of a paradox in this song. Everything changes and yet everything stays the same! Both can to be true at the same time. These ideas permeate many theological teachings. According to the lyrics, while Peter's health is deteriorating and ephemeral, the terrain that remains on his dying day appears immutable and ageless.

Impermanence is evident in Peter's ravaged body as his fever goes up and down. Conspicuously these kinds of changes are one of the profound essential doctrines of Buddhism. The teaching asserts that all existence changes. One interpretation of the Buddhists' First Noble Truth is that we suffer because we do not understand or fully grasp our own impermanence. Even though we pretend it ain't so, all temporal things are subject to Peter's fate, i.e. creation, decline, and destruction. Human life embodies this flux in the aging process. From birth to death, our bodies and minds transform and eventually diminish. We may lose our hair, strength, virility, teeth, mobility, eye sight, hearing, memory....you name it. These changes culminate finally when we draw our very last breath. (Afterwards a new cycle of change takes place on our residual dust.) Even with the assistance of top-notch medical technology and countless interventions, all living people will die. Death, just like birth (and taxes), is a natural part of the dynamic circle of life.

On the other end of the paradox, in the Judeo-Christian tradition, the continuity of the world and the vanity of human's effort to change it are expressed by the author of Ecclesiastes: "*What has been will be again, what has been done will be done again; there is nothing new under the sun*" (ECC. 1:9). Even after our heroic efforts to make a big difference, hug trees, save the whales, recycle it all, and usher in the Age of Aquarius, not much really changes in the world.

Regardless of my noble intentions, the world remains pretty much the same. Same old shit, recycled in new ways! Certainly, our human nature remains unbent. Even more poignant is the idea in the song that after all my vain efforts, at the pinnacle of my entire life—on the exact day I die—it will be like any other day that's ever been. On that day the sun will rise in the East and set in the West, as it has from the beginning of time. Truly mind blowing stuff!

With crazy wisdom, Louie C.K. alluded to both sides of the mystery of continuity and change in the following way, *"Lots of things happen after you die; just none of them include you.... There's all kinds of shit. There's the super bowl every year. There is a dog catching a frisbee."*[8] Much will happen in my absence. On the day I die, all of my appointments and plans will be irrelevant. My urgent text messages, emails, and phone calls will remain unanswered. My prized material possessions will be left in the hands of others to care for or discard. All the arguments that I've won will provide me no comfort. Every superficial worry about my hairline or waistline will subside. But, the sun will rise and set, just like always. In my opinion, Robert Hunter captured all of these profound sentiments in the simple lyrics of "Black Peter."

My take on this song supports the idea that the PRESENT is really all that matters. Peter's life was nearly over and his time on earth would be nothing but a memory for others. The future hadn't happened yet for him. But, best guesses are that after Peter's death, it will be just like any other day that's ever been. Our present time, like Peter's, is precious and fading with no guarantees for tomorrow. It is Peter's fleeting life, not his tombstone—that is most significant. His common desire for a little peace and fellowship with loved ones provides some rationale for me to get out of bed each morning. That yearning for companionship and contentment is both invigorating and life affirming. Therefore, even though not much will change after I'm gone, I still want to be an active player in each new day above ground. Hunter advocated playing the cards you're dealt in this game of life in other lyrics. After all, "...*you got to play your hand / sometime the cards ain't worth a dime / if you don't lay 'em down*" ("Truckin'"). I'll resist cashing in my chips early and, again and again, choose to play the game.

My life has been enriched by these insights. As a result, I am more comfortable with the concept of death than I'd be without this band's contribution to my consciousness. This song has provided particular meaning, if not comfort. It is a song that helps me better understand the feelings of the dying person.

Lessons learned from the Grateful Dead were a big part of my motivation to work as a hospice volunteer for several years. I had something both to offer and receive via my participation with terminal patients. As a result, I have witnessed death up close. Through the care-giver experience, like many hospice volunteers, I probably gained more than I gave. Hospice volunteers often say that being intimately involved with another person's death gives them a greater appreciation for life. Most report it makes them more grateful and less susceptible to getting ruffled over life's smaller hassles such as poor customer service and traffic jams.

By no means do I want to minimize the grief and hardships associated with the passing of others. I am well aware that death can be fully devastating for those still living. In addition to hospice clients, I have had friends, family, and other loved ones meet their demise. I too have experienced great sorrow in their wake. As I first wrote this, only today was I able to delete the phone number of a close friend who died over three years ago. Maintaining those digits somehow kept the memory of that person alive for me. Death can be hard, indeed. As I age, my familiarity with the closing curtains on life increases exponentially as more and more people I know draw closer to their expiration date. But, with some calmness I remind myself that it is a natural process. After a death, for those who remain, life continues. At the culmination of any life, Black Peter's or mine, the sun goes up and down as usual.

Recently my daughter asked me if I was afraid to die. I told her truthfully, *"no, I wasn't."* I don't wish to die right now. Like most of us, there are many, many, things I yet want to do and experience in this life. But, right now I am not frightened by the concept of my own departure. That seems to be a reasonable outlook for a relatively healthy man in the later years of his life. Perhaps as time passes and my biological hour glass dwindles, my view of my own death may change. But for the time being, like Peter when I reach the end of my days, I just want to have a little peace to die and a loved one or two at hand.

Chapter 11

"We will get by /
We will survive"

From "Touch of Grey" 1987
by Robert Hunter and Jerry Garcia

The song "Touch of Grey" has an odd history. Yet the
inspiring anthem, *"We will get by / We will survive,"* emerged
from this song. Apparently Robert Hunter began writing the
lyrics of the song in 1980 and the Dead first performed it in
1982. They played it only occasionally over the next few
years, and finally recorded it much later for their 1987 album
In The Dark. Although the song is still loved by most fans, it
was considered a mixed blessing for the band. After over two
decades together, this was the Dead's first and only commercial
hit song. "Touch of Grey" rose to number nine on the *Billboard
Hot 100* chart and remained there for fifteen weeks in 1987.

That same year, *MTV* debuted the Grateful Dead's first music video: "Touch of Grey." The video gained major airplay on *MTV* and featured a live performance of the band. In the video, life-size skeleton marionettes morphed into the actual band members playing their big hit. The popularity of the single and its video helped introduce the Grateful Dead to a new group of fans, resulting in the band gaining mainstream acclaim.

Dennis McNally recalled that when the band was told that "Touch of Grey" had hit the top ten, Jerry Garcia responded "*I am appalled*" (McNally, 2002, p. 566). Remember this was a band famous for eschewing most music business conventions. Live concerts were the band's super power. Studio recordings were regarded as little more than raw meat tossed to satisfy the cravings of the music industry crocodiles.[2] Yet, the band now experienced an unfamiliar level of acceptance. Following the release of "Touch of Grey" the Grateful Dead evolved from an underground cult-like band to a group with major mainstream cultural and financial success. Of course this was the same year, ice cream fans could enjoy a new flavor of Ben and Jerry's named "Cherry Garcia." After more than twenty years playing together, at long last the Grateful Dead was in vogue to the prevailing American public.

This newfound acclaim transformed the band and the fans as the Grateful Dead continued on their long strange trip. Basically, the band members joined the ranks of *nouveau riche* rockstars as the concert crowds exploded. During a press conference, a reporter asked in what ways did mainstream success change the Grateful Dead. Bob Weir downplayed the accidental mutation with this gem:

> *"I was noticing the other night, for instance, that when I'm going through pistachios, opening pistachios—the hard-to-open ones? I don't bother with them anymore"* (McNally, 2002, p. 567).

But changes to their audience could not be so easily dismissed.

While thousands totally "got" the Grateful Dead during this era and became lifelong fans, *"A crass new wave of concertgoers, naive to longstanding Deadhead behavioral norms were derisively dubbed 'Touchheads' by the old guard."*[2] Many of these Touchheads came to Dead shows just to party hardy—Yeehaw! To them, the music was far from their priority. Instead of going to Fort Lauderdale for a wild spring break, they opted to go on tour with the Dead. The number of people in the parking lot tripled. But many never ventured into the concert venue to hear the band.[3] Far too many acted like drunk frat-boys; obnoxious, aggressive, and mean—assholes to be precise.

During this era at a concert, I witnessed some dreadful conduct. I saw predatory young males ply nubile young teeny boppers with alcohol and hard drugs. The zombified girls later became easy prey, I suppose. In my opinion, this kind of behavior was previously atypical for Grateful Dead shows. But, it happened during Deadmania. Bad behavior and the swollen influx of new concert crowds led to legal, logistical, and security problems. Accordingly, the Dead was banned from a number of long-suffering venues and cities. Here was the mixed blessing of a "Touch of Grey." *"It was the hit that almost killed the band"* (McNally, 2002, p. 596).

The origin of this song makes it an unlikely host for positive affirmation. The song's history is quite ugly. Hunter explained the inception of the "Touch of Grey" this way:

> *"You know, I'll give you the blistering truth about it. A friend brought over a hunk of very good cocaine. I stayed up all night. And at dawn I wrote that song. That was the last time I ever used cocaine. Nor had I used it for many years before that. Now I listen to it and it's that attitude you get when you've been up all night speeding and you're absolutely the dregs. I think I got it down in that song."* [4]

Lyrically, the song was a superb snapshot of the morning after a cocaine binge. Apparently, the drug floods the brain with dopamine (the "feel good" neurotransmitter). The inevitable come down causes a dreary depression. Instead of enhancing the world's brilliant colors, the cocaine crash makes the world appear bland and colorless or "grey," at best. This doldrum is evident in these lyrics:

> *"Must be getting early /*
> *Clocks are running late /*
> *Paint by numbers morning sky /*
> *Looks so phony*
>
> *Dawn is breaking everywhere /*
> *Light a candle, curse the glare /*
> *Draw the curtains /*
> *I don't care /*
> *'Cause it's alright"*

The rest of the song includes a catalog of middle-age grumbles. The verses contain a litany of minor indignities and imperfect circumstances. There are complaints about unpaid rent, insolent teenagers, overly demanding relationships, and the sorry state of the world in general. What Dead Head over the age of 60 can't relate to that? The song is a melodic shake of the fist, in which you can almost hear a grouchy Robert Hunter scream, *"Hey you kids, get off my lawn!"* Just about everybody can connect to "Touch of Grey" on some level. But, most can't quite unravel all that weirdness in the verses about cows giving kerosene and the shoe being on the hand it fits.

Because of the song's background, the optimistic forecast of the song's chorus, *"We will get by / We will survive,"* is quite ironic. The song worked! Garcia explained that the original interpretation of the song was moot after the audience's embrace:

> *"It doesn't matter what it originally means anymore. I like to not tie things down if possible. That thing of floating… but it's a great song to sing. It's a great song to perform. It really works well."* [5]

It became a celebratory anthem. Stadiums full of thousands of fans with raised hands singing along, *"We will survive,"* proved Garcia's point. Like the Grateful Dead survived fickle music trends, near bankruptcy, the deaths of bandmates and crew, Disco, substance abuse, Jerry's diabetic coma, and other historic bummers, Dead Heads too could weather their personal storms. I have been one of those hopeful fans. The impact these lyrics have had on me is authentic.

"We will get by / We will survive"

The song "Touch of Grey" has been prophetic for the band and its fans. I write this 27 years after the death of Jerry Garcia. Notably, the Grateful Dead has continued to survive after the passing of their avatar in surprising ways. It is widely believed that in the most recent years the band has been more popular than ever.[6] There are more Dead Heads today than when Jerry played his last concert in 1995. Although the original members of the band continue to dwindle, the music never stopped and the fans of the music seem undeterred.

Perhaps the clearest indication of the Dead's ongoing relevance is the continuing success of the bands that play their music. In 2015 the surviving members of the band announced their final "Fare Thee Well" concerts in Chicago to celebrate 50 years of the Grateful Dead. Over half a million Dead Heads logged on to Ticketmaster to request limited tickets for the shows, which set a record for concert demand.[7] Due to the high volume, two more concerts were required and scheduled in Santa Clara to satisfy their huge audience. Since then, the reunion band known as Dead & Company with original members, Mickey Hart, Bill Kreutzmann, and Bob Weir, has produced enviable touring revenues, averaging $2.3 million per concert. All of their shows were near sell-outs in large arenas, amphitheaters and stadiums, with total tickets sales in 2020 approaching three million (Halperin, 2020). Other offshoot bands like Bob Weir and the Wolf Brothers, Phil Lesh and Friends, the Mickey Hart Band, Billy & the Kids, Joe Russo's

Almost Dead, and Dark Star Orchestra have all had major achievements in the live concert arena. All of those bands primarily interpret the classic catalog of Grateful Dead tunes in unique and interesting ways. Other bands highly influenced by the improvisational spirit of the Grateful Dead, like Widespread Panic, Phish, the String Cheese Incident, and many more, keep on drawing huge dedicated crowds across America. Furthermore, over 700 bands are now listed in a website dedicated to tracking Grateful Dead cover bands worldwide.[8] The Grateful Dead's vibe expands with each of their successes.

In my own town of Austin, a local tribute band, Deadeye, is a phenomena that attracts large devoted audiences to the music and vibes of the Grateful Dead. (The popularity of this cover band is surprising since this city is saturated with lots of good, original music.) Their concerts remind me of the first times I saw the Grateful Dead. Then I could still experience the passion of the music performed in a small venue. Up close today, I become part of an immersive energetic feedback loop between the young hometown musicians and the audience. My local cover band respectfully channels that original magic I witnessed over half a century ago.

As the Grateful Dead has survived, Dead Heads must also. However, the need for our positive affirmation appears greater each day. News from the national media about impending existential threats bombard us all. Indeed, nuclear war, climate change, pandemics, racial upheaval, tribal politics, growing totalitarianism are all incredibly frightening phenomena for anyone paying attention. Add to this scary stew declining health plus financial and relationship losses, that multiply with our age. These crises can cause some to curl up in a docile position to await death. We're enticed to become victims of our circumstances.

> **At particularly rough times lately, I've had to remind myself of the popular motto, *"my track record for getting through my worst days so far is 100%."* That chestnut is reinforced by the song "Touch of Grey," and especially the chorus, *"We will get by / We will survive."***

"Touch of Grey" recognizes the validity of misfortune and its negative consequences in our lives. Great spiritual traditions also affirm the same reality that all life requires adversity. This includes physical suffering like pain, injury, and illness. It also encompasses emotional discomfort, like anxiety, frustration, boredom, and depression. Such is life according to the clerics. *"Every silver lining's got a touch of grey,"* according to Robert

Hunter. David Gans recognized an inherent irony in the tune. According to him, the song's appeal is upbeat, but hardly overreaching. *"It's a lovely song in a funny way, because it's this sort of anthem to lowered expectations,"* says Gans. *"'We will get by' is not exactly a rallying cry. Contrast that to 'We are the champions of the world'"* (Hamilton, 2022).

So, if we can't escape the trials and tribulations of life, what is our option? We can choose our response to those problems. A popular preacher stated *"Life Is 10% What Happens to You and 90% How You React."*[9] I recognized the truth of that statement via a watershed encounter with someone who seemed less fortunate than myself. Many years ago, as I struggled to grow up, I met a fellow Dead Head who was involved in a terrible auto accident and became paralyzed, requiring 24-hour care. Often, I feared how I would react if our circumstances were reversed. Despite his injury, my friend was optimistic about life, with plans to attend medical school in his bright future. At the time, my dreary outlook made my own life appear far less promising. The contrast in our viewpoints could not have been greater. Because hardship does eventually hit us all, my friend was a living testament to the essential need for positive attitude, shoved right in my cynical face.

> **I learned there is no greater lesson for me than this: my happiness is my own choice. It is not other people, where I live, a bad haircut or other assorted minor debacles that mess up my life as they once could.**

My injured friend found happiness despite his broken body. Likewise, it was not my shifting fortune that should determine my satisfaction in life. "Touch of Grey" bolstered these ideas. Hunter implied this idea is as basic as *"the ABCs we all must face."* I cannot always choose my circumstances. But I can always choose my response and *"Try to keep a little grace."* No matter how bad it gets, along with my disabled friend I can shout out to the darkness, *"I will get by / I will survive."*

Despite unlikely odds, the Grateful Dead absorbed that message and survived for an extraordinary 50 years. That longevity was unusual for artists in the fickle music business. Remember the Beatles only lasted about eight years. But, I believe that some form of the Grateful Dead will live on for many years to come. It seems that the love of their music has eclipsed the adoration of the performers themselves. The vitality of the musical offshoots of the band, after all this time, may indicate that the real love of many Dead Heads was not directed at the celebrity bandmates but at the <u>music</u> and the <u>spirit</u> in which it was made. The musicians may come and go, but the music will survive. This was confirmed by a prophetic vision received by Bob Weir. In a dream, he supposedly saw the future of the Grateful Dead in which his fellow musicians were replaced by younger players. Weir stated, *"It made me realize that if we serve this legacy, it'll go on and people will teach this in music school in 200 or 300 years."*[10]

I too believe that hundreds of years from now, people will look back at the 20th century and discover something amazing was happening with this wonderful music and the fans who loved it. This durability will be based on the fact that the band has created something much larger than itself—an entire genre of Grateful Dead music.[11] Some will only embrace this style, fuse multiple musical traditions, and let improvisational jams be their guiding force, yet never play specific Grateful Dead tunes. Other future musicians will perform their own interpretations of standards from a classic Grateful Dead songbook, much like in the genres of blues and jazz. Indeed, the song "Touch of Grey" will be one of those standards. The simple affirmative words *"We will survive,"* will continue to cause goosebumps and lift the spirits of those who need it. It certainly works for me.

"Touch of Grey" captured a moment in time in the late 20th century that was full of challenges and disappointments for Robert Hunter and the Grateful Dead. But this song conveyed a sentiment of optimism despite their prevalent difficulties.

> **Notice the line in the song changed from the first person singular, "_I_ will survive," to the first person plural, "_We_ will survive." The message became more inclusive. Its intent expanded to both the band members and the Dead community as it served as a mantra of resilience.**

I have posted the printed lyrics of this song on my office wall for years. Those words have served as an inspiration during difficult times. Today, there is broad agreement about the power of the song. Whatever the circumstances now, the chorus can raise the spirits of those who hear it.

In June 2017, Dead & Company played a huge show at a sold-out Citi Field stadium in New York City. When they performed "Touch of Grey" as their encore, a light show on the Empire State Building was synchronized with the song. This dramatic display on that iconic building was further evidence of the universal appeal of both the band and the song. Despite the ongoing turmoil around us, the lyrics proclaim to me, all Dead

Heads, and the world, *"We will get by / We will survive!"* Thank God for the life-affirming wisdom of the Grateful Dead!

One final thought on survivability—my relationship with this music is extensive and enduring. I became a Dead Head (although the term was not coined until 1971), upon my first Grateful Dead concert. That was still the early era of acid tests, Captain Trips, and Pigpen. The crowd was small, the music was raw, and the new experiences were bewildering to this 16-year-old teenager. But there was something transformative about that original experience. The awe the music inspired in me then has lasted throughout my life. Despite being just a gobsmacked fanboy, I have loved this band for 55 years. Few things in my life have lasted so long. Shiny new cars have long ago rusted out. A marriage has come and gone. I moved to new houses several times. Friendships have faded. Even, the original band no longer exists. But, my love of the Grateful Dead and its music has endured.

As I enter my eighth decade on this planet, I've certainly been touched by grey in mostly unbecoming ways. Amazingly, the joy and inspiration I continue to receive from the Grateful Dead has survived. This music has changed my life for the better. Until my dying days, as a Dead Head I will raise my fist and loudly proclaim, *"We will survive."*

Epilogue

*"Would you hear my voice /
come through the music /
would you hold it near /
as it were your own?"*

From "Ripple" 1970
by Robert Hunter and Jerry Garcia

The Grateful Dead has been hailed as one of the most

impressive and influential American rock and roll bands of all

time. Ironically, their achievements occurred despite the fact

the Grateful Dead had been pronounced dead and buried

many times. In 1973, the charismatic frontman, Ron (Pigpen)

McKernan, passed. Subsequently, even Jerry Garcia assumed

the band would never fully recover. In 1995, 2,314 concerts

later, Jerry died at the young age of 53. At that time, the

remaining band members decided to bury the name "Grateful

Dead." In the leader's absence, their spin-off groups like

Ratdog, The Other Ones, the Dead, and Furthur revived sweet

but short-lived memories of the good ol' band. In 2015, the surviving musicians (Mickey Hart, Bill Kreutzmann, Phil Lesh, and Bob Weir) bid a final farewell to their fans. Five concerts, celebrating 50 years of Grateful Dead music, were publicized as the last time the core-four members would perform together. Most assumed those "Fare Thee Well" shows would put a stake through the heart of the band's succession. A month after waving goodbye to fans, three of those four musicians (Hart, Kreutzmann, and Weir) announced they'd be reconfiguring again in a new group called Dead & Company. Eight years later, on July 16, 2023, after 235 performances, Dead & Company once again threw in the towel. Could the summer of '23 with the final tour of the wildly popular spin-off band, Dead & Company, spell the ultimate epitaph of the Grateful Dead?

Premature obituaries for the band and its influence have been written many times. Now, almost three decades after the band called it quits following Garcia's death, the Grateful Dead's legacy and music seem more popular than ever. The evidence of endurance is everywhere.

In recent months, I attended a sold-out concert of Bob Weir and the Wolf Bros in Austin, Texas. Weir's new band interprets the beloved Dead songbook in novel ways, often adding a Wolfpack of improvisational horns and strings and an occasional full-blown orchestra to the mix. Future concerts of this band and other configurations have already been announced, as Bob Weir apparently intends to "*keep on truckin'*," into the future.

Annual celebrations are observed in the "Days Between," (the hallowed time frame between August 1st, Jerry's birthday, and August 9th, the date he passed away). Those days provide many fans and hundreds of Grateful Dead tribute bands the opportunity to pay homage to Garcia, in public venues all across the country. This Jerry holiday has become a time to contemplate all we've lost and to joyously celebrate our living memories, the Dead Head community, and the unique music of the band. "Days Between" is also the name of a gorgeous song, one of the last composed by Hunter and Garcia.

This year, the 13th local observance of Jerry Garcia's Birthday bash again took place in downtown Austin. I joined a packed crowd of multi-generational Dead Heads to enjoy the music respectfully performed by a great Austin cover band. This celebration of Jerry's birthday is like a national/religious holiday to me. Like Christmas, it marks time and I look forward to the special celebration all year long.

Another highly anticipated event takes place at movie theaters. The Grateful Dead was back for the 11th annual

"Meetup at the Movies." With new friends, I saw a previously unreleased film of a concert from Chicago, 1991. It was screened in select theaters worldwide and available in my hometown. At these movies, some folks actually dance in the aisles and cheer the performance as if they were present at the concert in real time.

All of these kinds of happenings in my locale keep the music of the Grateful Dead perpetually alive. A vibrant local community of fans provides year-round fellowship and fun at concerts, parties, and other special events. Many of my best friends in Austin, coincidentally, are Dead Heads.

National festivals also highlight Grateful Dead music. The "Skull and Roses Festival" takes place in Ventura, California and attracts folks from around the country. "Play Dead" happens in Concord, North Carolina. "The Grateville Dead Music Festival" is in Louisville, Kentucky. In Chicago, a festival called "Dancing in the Streets" pays its respect to the band. In Buffalo, New York, there is even a "Grateful Dead Laser Musical Experience" at a planetarium.

There are many more examples of these kinds of events. All around the country, people continue to come together to savor both the music and the vibe of this remarkable band.

Few other musical groups have these continuing and heartfelt accolades.

Other sources broadcast that the music of the Dead lives on. *The Grateful Dead Channel* was launched on SIRIUS Satellite Radio in 2007. Sixteen years later, the SXM channel (Ch. 23) features music spanning the band's career with unreleased concert recordings and original shows hosted by band members and others. I renewed my subscription to the broadcast in order to enjoy on-the-go commercial-free music from the band. Due to popular demand, in 2021 two new channels, *Dead Tracks* and *Dead Archive*, devoted to this music, were also added to their SXM lineup. The *Good Ol' Grateful Deadcast* is another audio outlet for the band. This weekly podcast explores the music and mythology behind the influential band.

Wherever I go, it seems I am in earshot of more music, news, and good gossip about the Grateful Dead. I am reminded of the humorous old bumper sticker, "*Who are the Grateful Dead and why do they keep following me?*" Their presence still seems to be everywhere.

New epic recordings are also commercially available to tickle the ears and lighten the pocket books of some fans. For the rare collector, professional compilations of live concert recordings are available for sale with some hefty price tags from Rhino records. For example, *In And Out Of The Garden: Madison Square Garden '81, '82, '83*, consisting of 17 CDs of live music is now priced at $179.98. Even more extreme, a set of 24 classic LP records of the band's performances in 1972 in London's Lyceum theater is the Dead's largest vinyl boxset so far. It is sold to the collector for $549.98. While most of the Grateful Dead's recordings are more modestly priced, these represent newly-released treasures which are narrowly marketed for more affluent fans. iTunes music currently has 91 Grateful Dead albums for sale, most are live recordings.

The Grateful Dead seems destined for immortality through the sale of other official merchandise. Dead logos of dancing bears, lightning bolts, and skeletons are on thousands of products. They are licensed to dozens of companies and now sold in stores, including Walmart and Saks Fifth Avenue. Fans can buy many items, from Crocs to skateboards, all stamped with band trademarks.

New business ventures also illustrate an on-going commercial appeal of the band. The Grateful Dead and Ben & Jerry's company have shared space in the hearts, minds, and stomachs of music and ice cream fans alike since 1987, when they launched their flavor, "Cherry Garcia." But, in the fall of

2023, they've introduced a prototype flavor inspired by Bob Weir. The new novelty flavor is called "Jack Straw Berry," (a salute to a song written by Weir and Hunter). The Grateful Dead and these entrepreneurs have made good business sense in the past. Likewise, this future flavor could be both profitable and a real hoot for the fans.

The band's internet presence continues. Official websites for both the Grateful Dead and the Garcia estate continue to offer goods and services to eager patrons. The official Grateful Dead website (dead.net) provides exclusive limited-edition recordings, breaking news of the band and community, a periodic almanac, and merchandise. Likewise, Garcia-centric recordings, apparel, and other related items for fans are sold via the official Jerry Garcia website (garciafamilyprovisions.com).

The *Internet Archive* (archive.org) is an American digital library developed in the '90s which provides free access to collections of digitized materials, including websites, software applications, music, and audio-visual materials. Since 2004, this archive became an ideal home for the Grateful Dead's live performances recorded by fans (tapers). At last count, the *Internet Archive* has over 17,578 recordings of Grateful Dead concerts for <u>free</u> access to researchers, historians, scholars, and the general public. It's a Dead Head's musical paradise!

The emergent academic field of Grateful Dead studies is as rich and surprising as the band on which it focuses. The 26th annual meeting of the Grateful Dead area of the Southwest Popular/American Culture Association took place in Albuquerque, New Mexico in March of 2023. This organization, "the Grateful Dead Scholars Caucus," explores issues and themes about the band involving a dozen disciplines and fields. Another academic group, the "Grateful Dead Studies Association," has been in existence since 2019. It is an organization of scholars, writers, and academic professionals who study the Grateful Dead phenomenon. More than 300 scholars representing 26 different disciplines have contributed to their studies, giving more than 500 conference papers and publishing dozens of books and articles.

The behemoth of the Dead's academic representation however, exists at the University of California, Santa Cruz. At that university, a Grateful Dead Archive is made up of many thousands of artifacts collected by members of the band over the course of decades. This archive exists to preserve, organize, and describe these materials for research and enjoyment by scholars, teachers, students, and fans. UC Santa Cruz also created the Grateful Dead Archive Online, where over 45,000 digitized items from the band are shared.

Perhaps one more reminder of the continuing relevance of the Grateful Dead can be seen in the current "psychedelic renaissance." Science is just now catching up to what many Dead Heads discovered over 50 years ago, *"when the bus came by"* and we got on ("That's It for the Other One"). Only in recent decades have medical professionals started to realize the class of psychedelic drugs, like LSD, can be useful in the treatment of mental health disorders and the enhancement of well-being even in <u>healthy</u> individuals. Legislation in multiple states have enacted laws decriminalizing certain substances and even legalizing psychedelic therapy. Since the early acid tests during their live performance, the Grateful Dead and their fans provided a relatively supportive environment for exploration with these psychoactive compounds. I believe my personal experiences sharing a psychedelic cup from a *"fountain that was not made by the hands of men,"* ("Ripple") has aided my own psychological health and informed many positive aspects of my life.

All of these hallmarks indicate the Grateful Dead lives on and their legacy appears to be written in stone. What a long strange trip it's been! There really was something unique about the scruffy underground band I witnessed decades ago, as a first generation Dead Head. That band's work has continued to deeply impact our culture and subsequent generations of music lovers. Their music still matters.

To my ears, the collaboration of Robert Hunter and Jerry Garcia produced the greatest and most dynamic songbook of any American rock band. In the lyrics of Grateful Dead songs, I've found important lessons about the nature of life and death. My own *"long strange trip"* ("Truckin'") has been illuminated by this wisdom. That brilliance shines like the gold of sunshine and is often in agreement with great spiritual traditions, as well as plain old common sense. I consider the lessons learned from these songs to be valuable like their counterpart in precious metal. Similar to gold ore, this wisdom continues to enrich my life. Its value has increased with time. To share these treasures with readers has been my privilege.

This book has only touched the surface of the band's wisdom. There are many other original songs in the Grateful Dead's huge catalog which could be included. There are too many other examples to list of great songs containing deep meaning. Some of their messages include themes already discussed here. Other insights from additional tunes are left for someone else to explore and write about. I invite you to listen to the music of this remarkable band. You may be surprised, as I

Life Lessons in their Songs

have been, to hear a voice come through the music. I hope you too will choose to hold it near, as if it were your own.

"Ripple in still water /

*when there is no pebble tossed /
nor wind to blow*

*Reach out your hand /
if your cup be empty /
If your cup is full /
may it be again*

*Let it be known /
there is a fountain /
that was not made /
by the hands of men"*

from "Ripple"

References

Prologue

1) Tamarkin, J. (2022, Aug. 1 reprint). *Jerry Garcia: The Relix interview (part 1)*. Relix. https://relix.com/articles/detail/the_relix_interview_jerry_garcia_part_i/

2) Carr, R. (2010). *Where all the pages are my days: Metacantric moments in deadhead lyrical experience.* In J. Tuedio (Ed.) & S. Spector (Ed.). The Grateful Dead in concert (pp. 107-117). Jefferson, North Carolina: McFarland & Co.

3) Hunter, R. (1993) *Box of rain: Lyrics 1965-1993*. London, England: Penguin Books.

4) Allen, S. (2014, Feb. 7). *Aces back to back: The history of the Grateful Dead (1965-2013)* (p. 58). USA: Outskirts Press.

5) Golsen, T. (2022, May 12). *The Grateful Dead song Robert Hunter called "my favorite".* Far Out Magazine. https://faroutmagazine.co.uk/the-grateful-dead-song-robert-hunter-called-my-favourite/

6) Browne, D., & Blistein, J. (2019, Sept. 24). *Robert Hunter, Grateful Dead collaborator and lyricist, dead at 78.* Rolling Stone. https://www.rollingstone.com/music/music-news/robert-hunter-grateful-dead-dead-889788/

7) Kreutzmann, B. & Eisen, B. (2015). *Deal: My three decades of drumming, dreams, and drugs with the Grateful Dead* (p. 138). New York, New York: St. Martin's Press.

8) Barlow, J. P. (2005). Afterword. In D. Dodd. *The complete annotated Grateful Dead lyrics: The 50th anniversary edition* (p. 420). New York, New York: Simon & Schuster.

Chapter 1

1) Wolfe, T. (1968). *The electric kool-aid acid test*. New York, New York: Picador.

2) Barnes, H. (1994, July 22). Live Dead-the Grateful Dead finally come back to St. Louis, bringing music and myth. *St. Louis Post-Dispatch.* (St. Louis, Mo.) , 72.

3) McNally, D. (2002) *A long strange trip*. New York, New York: Broadway Books.

4) Internet Archive. (1968, Jan.17). *Grateful Dead live at Carousel Ballroom 1968-01-17.* https://archive.org/details/gd1968-01-17.sbd.jeff.3927.shnf/ gd68-01-17d1t04.shn

5) Jarnow, J. (2017, May 23). *A user's guide to the Grateful Dead.* Pitchfork. https://pitchfork.com/features/lists-and-guides/10078-the-grateful-dead-a-guide-to-their-essential-live-songs/?page=2

6) Jarnow, J. (2016). *Heads.* New York, New York: DeCapo Press.

7) Trager, O. (1997). *The American book of the Dead.* New York, New York: Fireside.

8) Jackson, B. (1999). *Garcia: An American life.* New York, New York: Penguin Books.

Chapter 2

1) Goodman, F. (1989, Nov. 30). *Jerry Garcia: The Rolling Stone interview.* Rolling Stone p.54. https://www.rollingstone.com/feature/jerry-garcia-grateful-dead-talk-about-their-new-album-built-to-last-interview-1989-42861/. (reprinted in *On a Roll pp. 49-55. in Jerry Garcia Collectors Edition. (2020). Rolling Stone.).

2) Schools, D. (Host). (2010, April 28), *I'm a bass player but what are you? Dave Schools interviews Phil Lesh.* Relix. https://relix.com/articles/detail/i-m-a-bass-player-but-what-are-you-dave-schools-interviews-phil-lesh/

3) DeLong, M. (1970, April 30). Magic exists...Grateful Dead stun crowd. *Colorado Springs Sun.* reprinted In Dead.Net. https://www.dead.net/archives/1970/clippings/article-colorado-springs-sun

4) James, W. (1902). *The variety of religious experience.* London, England: Longmans, Green & Co.

5) Adams, R. G. & Sardiello, R. (2000). *Deadhead social science.* Walnut Creek, Ca.: AltaMira Press.

6) Sylvan, R. (2002). *Traces of the spirit.* New York, New York: New York University Press.

7) Lennon, J. (1970, Dec.11). God [Lyrics], *John Lennon / Plastic Ono Band.* London: United Kingdom: Apple Records.

8) Marre, J. (Producer). (1999). *Classic albums–The Grateful Dead: Anthem to Beauty* [DVD]. Rhino/WEA.

9) McNally, D. (2002). *A long strange trip.* New York, New York: Broadway Books.

10) Browne, D. (2015, March 9). *Robert Hunter on Grateful Dead's early days, wild tours,'sacred' songs.* Rolling Stone. https://www.rollingstone.com/feature/robert-hunter-on-grateful-deads-early-days-wild-tours-sacred-songs-37978/5/

11) Meriwether, N. (2015, Oct. 29). *Documenting the Dead: Joseph Campbell and the Grateful Dead.* Dead.Net. https://www.dead.net/features/blog/documenting-dead-joseph-campbell-and-grateful-dead

12) Kesey, K. (1971, Jan. 1). The Bible. In P. Krassner & K. Kesey (Eds.). *The Last Supplement to the Whole Earth Catalog* (pp. 3-5). Menlo Park, Ca.: Whole Earth Catalog.

Chapter 3

1) Brokaw, T. (1998). *The greatest generation.* New York, New York: Random House.

2) Kornfield, J. (2000). *After the ecstasy the laundry: How the heart grows wise on the spiritual path.* London, England: Bantam Press.

3) Dass, R. (2000). *Still here: Embracing aging, changing, and dying.* New York, New York: Riverhead Books.

Chapter 4

1) Bailey, D. (June 28, 2021). *Improvisation in music program 4: Nothin' Premeditated* [Video]. In Jeremy Marre (Dir.) On the Edge, February 23, 1992. https://www.youtube.com/watch?v=oOx2lo4fqBE.(Original work 1992, Feb. 23)

2) McNally, D. (2002). *A long strange trip.* New York, New York: Broadway Books.

3) Ganns, D. (Host). (1989, June 12). *Interview with David Crosby.* Grateful Dead our no. 41. Dead.Net. http://www.dead.net/features/grateful-dead-hour-no-41

4) Lambert, G. (Host). (2013, Oct. 21). *Dead world roundup – talkin' with Phil.* Dead.Net. http://www.dead.net/features/dead-world-roundup/dead-world-roundup-talkin-phil

5) Carlson, T. (Host), (2005, May 9). *Tucker Carlson interviews Phil Lesh of the Grateful Dead.* Tucker Carlson: Unfiltered - Show # 145C1.

6) Wenner, J. & Reich, C. (2013, July 4). *The Rolling Stone interview: Jerry Garcia, part I.* Rolling Stone. https://www.rollingstone.com/feature/jerry-garcia-1972-interview-charles-reich-jann-wenner-849548/. (Original work published 1972).

7) Rivera, G. (Host) (1981, Dec. 10). *Jerry Garcia interview to Geraldo Rivera.* NBC 20/20.

8) Scott, D. M. & Halligan, B. (2010). *Marketing Lessons from the Grateful Dead: What every business can learn from the most iconic band in history.* Hoboken, New York: John Wiley and Sons.

9) United States Marine Corps. (n.d.). *Adapting to protect our nations future.* https://www.marines.com/explore-the-corps/shifting-threats/adapt.html

10) Dass, R. (n.d.). *I crochet.* Love Serve Remember Foundation. https://www.ramdass.org/i-crochet/

11) Kotler, S. (2014, Feb. 25), *Flow states and creativity.* Psychology Today. https://www.psychologytoday.com/us/blog/the-playing-field/201402/flow-states-and-creativity

12) Flow Genome Project (n.d.).*Boost your resilience, cognitive capacity, and impact in the world.* Flow Genome Project. https://www.flowgenomeproject.com/

13) Scinto, J. (2014, June 27). *Why improv training is great business training.* Forbes. https://www.forbes.com/sites/forbesleadershipforum/2014/06/27/why-improv-training-is-great-business-training/#1298718e6bcb

Chapter 5

1) Dodd, D. (2014, Jan. 16). *Greatest stories ever told-"Scarlet Begonias".* Dead.Net. https://www.dead.net/features/greatest-stories-ever-told/greatest-stories-ever-told-scarlet-begonias

2) Kreutzmann, B. & Eisen, B. (2015). *Deal: My three decades of drumming, dreams, and drugs with the Grateful Dead.* New York, New York: St. Martin's Press.

3) Watts, A. (n.d.). *The Chinese farmer...maybe.* Alan Watts Organization. https://alanwatts.org/chinese-farmer/ (audio recording).

4) Dolan, E. W. (2016, Aug. 30). *Study: 'Bad Trips' from mushrooms often result in improved sense of well-being.* PsyPost. http://www.psypost.org/2016/08/study-bad-trips-from-magic-mushrooms-often-result-in-an-improved-sense-of-personal-well-being-44684

5) *The story of a man who was fired for a lack of creativity but went on to build his own empire.* (n.d.). Bright Side. https://brightside.me/wonder-people/the-story-of-a-man-who-was-fired-for-a-lack-of-creativity-but-went-on-to-build-his-own-empire-798520/

6) Sylvan, R. (2002). *Traces of the spirit.* New York, New York: New York University Press.

Chapter 6

1) Edelstein, J. (2021, May 5). *And now, the definitive EV ranking of gambling songs by the Grateful Dead.* USBets, https://www.usbets.com/grateful-dead-gambling-songs/

2) Dodd, D. (2014, Oct. 2). *Greatest stories every told-"Loser".* Dead.Net. https://www.dead.net/features/greatest-stories-ever-told/greatest-stories-ever-told-loser

3) Iacurci, G. (2022, Feb. 22). *Consumers lost $5.8 billion to fraud last year — up 70% over 2020.* CNBC. https://www.cnbc.com/2022/02/22/consumers-lost-5point8-billion-to-fraud-last-year-up-70percent-over-2020.html

4) Rothschild, M. (2018, Nov. 19). *Atrocious things that happened because of Bernie Madoff.* Ranker. https://www.ranker.com/list/bernie-madoff-scandal-casualties/mike-rothschild

5) Konnikova, M. (2016). *The confidence game: Why we fall for It...every time.* New York, New York: Penguin Random House.

6) Klosowsky, T. (2022, May 26). How to block spam calls. *New York Times.* https://www.nytimes.com/wirecutter/guides/how-to-stop-spam-calls/

Chapter 7

1) Eisenhart, M. (1987, Nov. 12). *Jerry Garcia interview (part 2 of 4).* http://www.yoyow.com/marye/garcia2.html

2) Gibney, A. & Elwood, A. (2011). In *Magic Trip: Ken Kesey's search for a kool place* (video). Magnolia Pictures.

3) Cutler, S. (2017). Act Two—This is now, In Amir Bar-Lev [producer]. *Long Strange Trip* (video)., Amazon Studios.

4) Brightman, C. (1998). *Sweet chaos: The Grateful Dead's American adventure.* New York, New York: Pocket Books.

5) Brand, S. (1971). *Last whole earth catalog.* New York, New York: Random House.

6) Richardson, P. (2015). Ecstasy. In *No simple highway: A cultural history of the Grateful Dead* (pp. 9-146). New York, New York: St. Martin's Press.

7) Eisenhart, M. (1987, Nov. 12). *Jerry's brokedown palaces interview 11/12/87.* San Francisco, Ca.:One Pass Studios http://jerrygarciasbrokendownpalaces.blogspot.com/2012/12/mary-eisenhart-interview-111287-one.html

8) Goodman, F. (1989, Nov. 30). *Jerry Garcia: The Rolling Stone interview.* Rolling Stone p. 54. https://www.rollingstone.com/feature/jerry-garcia-grateful-dead-talk-about-their-new-album-built-to-last-interview-1989-42861/. (reprinted in *On a Roll pp. 49-55. in Jerry Garcia Collectors Edition (2020) Rolling Stone.).

9) Dodd, D. (2005), *The complete annotated Grateful Dead lyrics.* New York, New York: Simon & Schuster. p. 218

10) Wendell, P. (2015, June 26). *"U.S. Blues" – The Dead's ode to the counterculture.* Songmango. http://songmango.com/u-s-blues-the-deads-ode-to-the-counterculture/

11) Browne, D. (2015, March 9). *Robert Hunter on Grateful Dead's early days, wild tours, 'Sacred' songs.* Rolling Stone. https://www.rollingstone.com/feature/robert-hunter-on-grateful-deads-early-days-wild-tours-sacred-songs-37978/

12) Hensley, G. (2005, May 9). *Tucker Carlson interviews Phil Lesh of the Grateful Dead.* Strategic Media Content & Platforms. http://www.dcspectator.com/tucker-carlson-interviews-phil-lesh-of-the-grateful-dead/

13) McNally, D. (2015). *Jerry on Jerry: The unpublished Jerry Garcia interviews* (ebook edition). New York, New York:Black Dog & Levanthal Publishers.

14) Schwarz. H. (2015, July 1). Grateful Dead fans: Surprisingly Republican, *Washington Post.* https://www.washingtonpost.com/news/the-fix/wp/2015/07/01/grateful-dead-fans-surprisingly-republican/?utm_term=.580335490649

15) Avlon, J. P. (2005, Aug. 9). *Jerry Garcia, the Grateful Dead, and the Republicans who love them.* Strategic Media Content & Platforms. https://www.strategicmedia.net/jerry-garcia-the-grateful-dead-and-the-republicans-who-love-them/

16) Watch Dead & Company get interviewed by Anderson Cooper and Andy Cohen on New Year's Eve (2020, Jan.1). Jambands.com. https://jambands.com/news/2020/01/02/watch-dead-company-get-interviewed-by-anderson-cooper-and-andy-cohen-on-new-years-eve/

17) Barnes, B. (2011). *Everything I know about business I learned from the Grateful Dead* (pp. 92-93). New York, New York: Grand Central Publishing.

Chapter 8

1) Shalit, A. (1995). *Roll away the dew: An exegesis of Robert Hunter's "Franklin's Tower".* http://artsites.ucsc.edu/gdead/agdl/shalit.html

2) Hunter, R. (1996, March 4). *Fractures of unfamiliarity & circumvention in pursuit of a nice time.* http://artsites.ucsc.edu/GDead/agdl/fauthrep.html

3) Dodd, D. (2014, Feb 27). *Greatest stores ever told-"Franklin's Tower".* Dead.Net. https://www.dead.net/features/greatest-stories-ever-told/greatest-stories-ever-told-franklins-tower

4) Barnes, T. (2014, Aug. 14). *There's a "Magic Age" when you find your musical taste, According to Science.* MIC. https://www.mic.com/articles/96266/there-s-a-magic-age-when-you-find-your-musical-taste-according-to-science

5) Jackson, A. G. (2018, July 10). *1965: The most revolutionary year in music.* New York, New York: MacMillan Publishers.

6) Beech, S. (2022, Mar. 9). *Listening to music really does chill people out, reduces anxiety.* StudyFinds.https://www.studyfinds.org/listening-to-music-anxiety/

7) Szalavitz, M. (2012, Dec. 26). *Unlikely partners: Grateful Dead drummer teams with scientist to study how rhythm heals.* Time. https://healthland.time.com/2012/12/26/unlikely-partners-grateful-dead-drummer-teams-with-scientist-to-study-how-rhythm-heals/

8) Hart, M. (2012, Sept. 7). *Mickey Hart discusses healing nature of music on PBS 'NewsHour'* [Video]. Live for Live Music. https://liveforlivemusic.com/news/mickey-hart-pbs-newshour-drone-music/#:~:text=Hart's%20work%20with%20the%20medical,himself%20as%20a%20test%20subject

9) Kennedy, R. (n.d.). *The power of music.* https://firingthemind.com/psychoanalysis/power-of-music/

10) *Beatles 'brought down communists'* (2021, Mar. 23). BBC. http://news.bbc.co.uk/2/hi/entertainment/1235862.stm

Chapter 9

1) Mather, A. (2013, July 9). *10/7/13 – Robert Hunter.* https://thewilbur.com/robert-hunter-the-wilbur-october-7th/

2) Barlow, J. P. (2011). Foreward. In B. Barnes. *Everything I know about business I learned from the Grateful Dead* (pp. xvii-xxxii). New York, New York: Business Plus

3) Deadhead. (2023, Aug. 22). In *Wikipedia.* https://en.wikipedia.org/wiki/Deadhead

4) Harrington, J. (2015, June 23). *The Grateful Dead-Reagan connection: How two California icons spurred a social phenomenon in the 1980s.* Bay Area News Group. http://www.mercurynews.com/2015/06/23/the-grateful-dead-reagan-connection-how-two-california-icons-spurred-a-social-phenomenon-in-the-1980s/

5) McNally, D. (2012, Aug. 1). *My Jerry: Dennis McNally remembers Jerry Garcia.* Relix. https://relix.com/articles/detail/my-jerry-dennis-mcnally-remembers-jerry-garcia/

6) Hockman, S. (1991, May 25). Grateful Garcia: His archetypal '60s group Is more popular than ever. *LA Times.* https://www.latimes.com/archives/la-xpm-1991-05-25-ca-2116-story.html

7) Clinton, B (1995, Aug.12). *Former President Bill Clinton on Jerry Garcia's death* [Video]. Youtube. https://www.youtube.com/watch?v=GXjHwAnHepM

8) Giles, J. (2015, July 24). *The Grateful Dead's fare thee well shows made a whole bunch of money.* Ultimate Classic Rock. https://ultimateclassicrock.com/grateful-dead-fare-thee-well-money/?utm_source=tsmclip&utm_medium=referral https://ultimateclassicrock.com/grateful-dead-fare-thee-well-money/

9) Kreps, D. (2015, July 5). *Obama pens tribute to iconic Grateful Dead.* Rolling Stone. https://www.rollingstone.com/music/music-news/barack-obama-pens-tribute-to-iconic-grateful-dead-35143/

10) Grateful Dead tribute bands. Retrieved Sept. 22, 2023, from http://www.gratefuldeadtributebands.com/

11) David A. (2018, Feb. 19). *Inspiration move me brightly.* Gratefulweb. https://www.gratefulweb.com/articles/inspiration-move-me-brightly

12) Olinga, L. (2023, Feb. 11). *Bill Gates reveals the next big thing.* The Street. https://www.thestreet.com/technology/bill-gates-reveals-the-next-big-thing

13) Fleming, S. (2019, July 16). *What telephones and television can teach us about the adoption of broadband.* Microsoft. https://news.microsoft.com/on-the-issues/2019/07/16/telephones-television-adoption-broadband/

Chapter 10

1) Jackson, B. (2000). *Garcia: An American life.* London, England: Penguin Books.

2) Richardson, P. (2015). *No simple highway: The cultural history of the Grateful Dead.* New York, New York. St. Martin's Press.

3) O'Neill, A. (2022, June 21). *Life expectancy (from birth) in the United States, from 1860 to 2020.* Statista. https://www.statista.com/statistics/1040079/life-expectancy-united-states-all-time/

4) Shumway, E. (2021, Sept. 29). *Why it may be time for a more compassionate bereavement policy.* HRDive. https://www.hrdive.com/news/why-it-may-be-time-for-a-more-compassionate-bereavement-policy/607374/

5) Songs played total. Setlist.fm. https://www.setlist.fm/stats/grateful-dead-bd6ad4a.html

6) Wendell, P. (n.d.), *Smoldering versions of 'Black Peter'.*Songmango. http://songmango.com/dead-best-7-smoldering-versions-of-black-peter/

7) Dodd, D. (2013, May 23). *Greatest stories ever told-'Black Peter'*. Dead. Net. http://www.dead.net/features/greatest-stories-ever-told/greatest-stories-ever-told-black-peter

8) Stuever, H. (2014, May 4). FX's 'Louie' and the blundering wisdom that comes with age. *Washington Post*. https://www.washingtonpost.com/entertainment/tv/fxs-louie-and-the-blundering-wisdom-that-comes-with-age/2014/05/04/226d47cc-d0ab-11e3-937f-d3026234b51c_story.html?utm_term=.ccf1c978af94

Chapter 11

1) McNally, D. (2005). *A long strange trip*. New York, New York: Broadway Books.

2) Hamilton, K. (2022, July 22). *Grateful Dead "Touch of Grey" meaning*. Esquire. https://www.esquire.com/entertainment/music/a40601133/grateful-dead-touch-of-grey-meaning/.

3) Jackson, Blair, (2012, June 12). *Blair's golden road blog-that "touch of Grey" summer*. Dead.Net. https://www.dead.net/features/blair-jackson/blair-s-golden-road-blog-touch-grey-summer.

4) Browne, D. (2015, Mar. 11). *Grateful Dead's Robert Hunter on Jerry's final days: 'We Were Brothers'*. Rolling Stone. https://www.rollingstone.com/music/music-news/grateful-deads-robert-hunter-on-jerrys-final-days-we-were-brothers-97334/3/.

5) Kreutzmann J. (Director). (1987). *Dead Ringers: The Making of the Touch of Grey Video* (VHS) [Film], 6 West Home Video: Arista.

6) Halperin, S. (2020, Aug. 6). *25 years after Jerry Garcia's death, the Grateful Dead Is bigger than ever*. Variety. https://www.yahoo.com/entertainment/25-years-jerry-garcia-death-175430604.html.

7) Fare Thee Well: Celebrating 50 years of the Grateful Dead. (2023, May 12). In *Wikipedia*. https://en.wikipedia.org/wiki/Fare_Thee_Well:_Celebrating_50_Years_of_the_Grateful_ Dead

8) Grateful Dead tribute bands. Retrieved Sept. 22, 2023, from http://www.gratefuldeadtributebands.com/

9) Swindoll, C. (2023, Jan. 17). *Life is 10% what happens to you and 90% how you react*. Nashville, Tn.: Thomas Nelson Inc.

10) Weir, B. (2016, Oct. 25). *Bob Weir talks heroes, dreams and visions*. Relix. https://relix.com/news/detail/bob_weir_talks_heroes_dreams_and_visions/

11) Conners, P., (2013) *JAMerica: The history of the jam band and festival scene*. Boston, Ma.: De Capo Press.

Attributions for Adobe Stock Images

Attributions for usage of licensed Adobe Stock Images (stock. adobe.com) within the book are included here. Page numbers are listed where Adobe assets reside in the book. Authors are attributed to copyrighted artwork on the referenced page(s).

pp i, 1,17, 35,49, 67, 85, 99, 117,133, 149, 163, 177 tatyana olina & Gizele/stock.adobe.com
p. x vectortatu/stock.adobe.com
p. 13 photosvac/stock.adobe.com
p. 20 daniilantig2010 & data_design/stock.adobe.com
p. 27 data_design/stock.adobe.com
p. 34 Nikolai Sorokin/stock.adobe.com
p. 36 berdsigns/stock.adobe.com
p. 38 Gizele & Casoalfonso/stock.adobe.com
p. 41 HappyRichStudio/stock.adobe.com
p. 48 berdesigns/stock.adobe.com
p. 50 helivideo/stock.adobe.com
p. 57 photosvac/stock.adobe.com
p. 65 Casoalfonso & Evgenia Pichkur/stock.adobe.com
p. 84 theogott/stock.adobe.com
p. 86 berdsigns/stock.adobe.com
p. 91 Evgenia Pichkur/stock.adobe.com
p..97 Christos Georghiou/stock.adobe.com
p.100 Kirill Semenov /stock.adobe.com
p.106 AllessandroDellaTorre/stock.adobe.com
p.115 Christos Georghiou/stock.adobe.com
p.116 SASINA N./stock.adobe.com
p.118 agrus/stock.adobe.com
p.120 rabbit75_fot/stock.adobe.com
p.126 artbalitskiy/stock.adobe.com
p.144 rockindaddy/stock.adobe.com
p.148 kolonko/stock.adobe.com
p.150 angela0982/stock.adobe.com
p.151 XAVIERDESIGN/stock.adobe.com
p.156 AlienCat/stock.adobe.com
p.168 OMIA/stock.adobe.com
p.187 Christos Georghiou/stock.adobe.com
p.188 hiro.y/stock.adobe.com

About the Author

Charles Beard

Charles has been a Grateful Dead fan for over 55 years. Since he attended a life-changing concert early in the Dead's career, he has been what was described later as a "Dead Head." As a result, he has adored the music of the Grateful Dead for most of his life. Their songs have made a deep and positive impact on his own "*long strange trip*."

The author has three daughters, who are his greatest source of pride. As a graduate of Texas State University, Harding School of Theology, and Texas A&M University, he received both undergraduate and graduate degrees. After working in Information Technology for over 30 years, he is now retired in Austin, Texas. He remains a strong supporter of the music scene and the Dead Head community in this vibrant town, known as the "Live Music Capital of the World."

Charles may be contacted at: goldenwisdombook@gmail.com

Made in the USA
Coppell, TX
25 November 2024

40995867R00132